Nature

A Treatise of Philosophy

KHURRAM MALIK

SKRYCOFT PUBLISHING

ISBN: 979-8-853430-1-50

"But let one man read another by his actions never so perfectly, it serves him onely with his acquaintance, which are but few. He that is to govern a whole Nation, must read in himself, not this, not that particular man; but Man-kind; which though it be hard to do, harder than to learn any Language, or Science; yet, when I shall have set down my own reading orderly, and perspicuously, the pains left another, will be onely to consider, if he also not find the same in himself, for this kind of Doctrine, admitteth of no other Demonstration."

Introduction by Hobbes to *Leviathan*

"TO THE HAPPY FEW"

Stendhal's *l'envoi* to his readers, in *his* work

Though the present treatise is self-contained, it follows, in philosophical order, taken historically, the principles *discovered*, of *ethics*, by *Hobbes* in the first quarter of *Leviathan*, the principles that "good" is an individual's self-interests, that "evil" is what hinders or gives pain to the advancement of those interests—an idea repeated, by examples, but not gone beyond, by Friedrich Nietzsche, when he notes that religious "Good" is like Plato's "Good": merely what founders of religions, or secular philosophers such as Plato, decided on as *what they wished to be considered good*, what pleased them, for political or scholarly purposes, and called those personal goods, "the Good."

Hobbes began and *almost* finished the branch of philosophy termed Ethics, called so because of Aristotle's classification near the beginning of western philosophy, though Aristotle, too, did not provide a psychological basis for ethics, as Hobbes was to do for the first time, but presented his own "medium" good as Good.

As for Politics, another branch of philosophy so designated, for the same reason, it has perhaps its first modern founder in Locke's *Second Treatise of Government*, though *both* Hobbes, in originating the social contract idea, and John Milton, with his proposition that absolute freedom of thought be granted to all individuals by the state, in his *Areopagitica, must* be considered *the founders of political philosophy.*

It was left to the French "novelist," Stendhal, to round out ethics and resolve the conflict between Milton's, Locke's, and Hobbes' views of political activity, in his novel, *The Red and the Black*, which, if read well, is actually a treatise *with narrative,* like Plato's dialogues, but much superior in treatment of the subject: viz. and e.g., royalists versus liberals, the Mayor of the protagonist Julien's town, is a royalist, born aristocrat, M. de Rênal, who, in time, as politics and the perceived "good" change, becomes the *liberal* main opposition rival to the new royalist Mayor, Valenod, a low-born and base opportunist, who has climbed his way to the top of the royalist "ticket" in that town, Verrières.

I say all this, to tell my readers that should they be looking for *a full exposition of ethics and politics,* they should turn to the works mentioned above, with *The Red and the Black* as the summit of world philosophy as it has existed heretofore.

*Stendhal himself on the subject of **philosophy*** [mine would be from an event from my life: when I was seeking employment in the U.S. in 199-, one firm I applied to "coached" students for SAT and GRE tests then popular for college and university admissions, and when they learned from my get-the-job advertising pitch that I was well-read in philosophic literature, they suggested strongly that though I had myself had a nearly perfect SAT score from sixteen years earlier, and a 97 percentile score for literature specialty GRE, I teach pre-law specialized tests instead of the general test, because, they said, "law and philosophy are essentially related professions." Word-parsing. One can see, from the weasliness of "legal analysts" on tv, former lawyers or prosecutors analyzing legal technicalities for networks, to elucidate them for the network's audience, that this is true—one *refreshing* exception to this is Mr. Elie Honig on one network whose name I forget. He lays the matters out *always* with *clearly* delineated, impartial, and politically uncharged attitude.] (from his article, signed as written by "Alcéste" (i.e., Molière's *Misanthrope*, in his play with the latter as title) for *Paris Monthly Review*, June 1822 issue, called "An Account of Kant's Philosophy," translated here by Geoffrey Strickland, and to be found in a volume edited by the last, titled "Selected Journalism from the English Reviews by Stendhal with translations of other Critical Writings, p. 153-155):

"While I was exercising my corpulent body, walking over the hillsides of Andilly and Montmorency, I plunged into German philosophy and have become completely *Kantified*…. I am sending you a *Short Course in Philosophy*, this being nothing more than the assembled notes of a recluse….

"Kant himself was not always clear as to his own meaning and it is extremely difficult for anyone else to follow it. When one has at last succeeded, one is left with truths so evident that they seem scarcely worth the trouble of pronouncing in the first place. These truths are mixed up with an immense heap of absurdities that a man of Kant's talent would never have uttered if the language he used had been more lucid.

"Nothing is more conducive to good philosophy than a language, which by its very nature, is necessarily clear. A man who is obscure in French, for instance, can have no illusions; either he is deceiving himself, or seeking to deceive someone else….

"All systems of philosophy are addressed to the young. Those philosophers whose self-respect is not too susceptible write what are, in reality, novels for delightful young people to applaud with all the enthusiasm one has at the age of twenty for a good novel. This was the secret of Plato's success in Athens, of Abélard's in Paris during the twelfth century, and today, once again in Paris, of the success of a young highly talented professor [Victor Cousin, the translator provides in a helpful footnote].

"I am now sixty years old and have read through every system of philosophy. I shall therefore write down thirty lines or so which I hope will be read by the young who are the hope of the nation.

"There are really only two sciences [at this point, Stendhal himself placed a footnote in the article: "A better word would be *art*. As art always depends on a science; it is the putting into practice the methods indicated by a science."] that a man can learn. The first of these is the science of knowing the motives of men's actions. As soon as you know men's true motives, you will be able to seek to cultivate in them other motives which will lead them to act in such a way as is likely to lead them to bring about your own happiness.

"Today, in 1822 [today, in 2022, "scientific" pollsters ask people to tell them, what is your personal opinion, which political party do you support, what is your favorite kitchen cleaner? Do you prefer coffee (or sex) in the morning or in the afternoon, and academic "psychologists" publish "scholarly" articles and "bestselling" books, based on such *reliable* evidence! And *policies* in private and public firms are modulated according to *these*.], men nearly always lie when they talk of their true motives. The most useful science for a young man, the science which at the age of twenty gives the clearest proof of intelligence, is that of penetrating lies of this kind. True politics are nothing more than the art of ensuring that Mr. Q— does not find his happiness in acting in a way that will harm Mr. B—. There is a book whose title ought to be *The Art of Discovering Men's True Motives*. This book is *De l'Esprit* by Helvétius. [Of course, that book, contrary to Stendhal's assertion here, had not yet been written, and it is called THE RED AND THE BLACK: Julien Sorel's so-called "hypocrisy"—the true *small-time* hypocrite is Molière's even more renowned Tartuffe, so much so that, even out of French-language culture, Tartuffe is synonymous with the idea of hypocrisy—is but *the universal application of that principle of all politics consists of* that has just been outlined in expository manner by Stendhal: "True politics are nothing more than the art of ensuring that all the Messrs. Q— in the world do not find their happiness in acting in a way that will harm Mr. Sorel."] ....

"I thus reduce *philosophy* to not misunderstanding the motives of men's actions, and to making no error in one's reasoning, or in the art of advancing towards happiness."

This was written by the author of *The Red and the Black* less than a decade before he published that novel.

I

1

Milton: The Two Christian Gods *Justified*

Paradise Lost begins,

Of Mans First Disobedience, and the Fruit
Of that Forbidden Tree, whose mortal tast
Brought Death into the World, and all our woe,
With loss of *Eden*, till one greater Man
Restore us, and regain the blissful Seat,
Sing Heav'nly Muse, that on the secret top
Of *Oreb*, or of *Sinai*, didst inspire
That Shepherd, who first taught the chosen Seed,
In the Beginning how the Heav'ns and Earth
Rose out of *Chaos*: Or if *Sion* Hill
Delight thee more, and *Siloa*'s Brook that flow'd
Fast by the Oracle of God; I thence
Invoke thy aid to my adventrous Song,
That with no middle flight intends to soar
Above th' *Aonian* Mount, while it pursues
Things unattempted yet in Prose or Rhime.
And chiefly Thou O Spirit, that dost prefer
Before all Temples th' upright heart and pure,
Instruct me, for Thou know'st; Thou from the first
Wast present, and with mighty wings outspread
Dove-like satst brooding on the vast Abyss
And mad'st it pregnant: What in me is dark

Illumine, what is low raise and support;
That to the highth of this great Argument
I may assert Eternal Providence,
And justifie the wayes of God to men.

It was to be John Milton's *singular* fate to cleanse christianity of its moral blather.

The first two books of his epic have been rightly praised and are impossible to overpraise, but the last three books of *Paradise Lost* are as bravura, but on an intellectual, temporal (since History now exists after, and because of, the First Couple's fall) and fullhuman rather than narrative and background atmosphere scale of the first two. Since this is a matter of *difficult thinking*, the end sequence of the poem does not seem to have been considered a high watermark point even by the Romantics, etc.

Milton: *Paradise Lost* as the ultimate poem, "a poem which ... with respect to design may claim the first place, and with respect to performance, the second, among the productions of the human mind" (at another point, *Paradise Lost* "is not the greatest of heroic poems, only because it is not the first"): among all poems, according to Samuel Johnson, the indispensable literary critic in the language (his masterpiece: *Lives of the Poets*, a work, I think, suggested to him by a publisher (I may be wrong) outstanding for its unerring nerve in taking on the greatest: on Milton, "Lycidas" which *he* thought insincere, and on Shakespeare, he is like Nabokov on Joyce and Tolstoy: maddening but never discountable) until Joyce and Nabokov: — it seems unlikely that the poet of the Commonwealth could get into the spirit of degrading Eve *and* Satan, and the devolving of the rebel angels into snakes is the one instance of commonality between Milton and Dante, in the serpent scene in *Inferno*, where Milton is slightly bettered. I speak a slightly canny curve: Dante is only great in his imagery (his characters all speak in the same manner, "By the great river that tears the Lucian mountains into halves was my birthplace" type of thing); Milton thinks and ponders and delves and comes rising out. In *Paradise Regain'd* Jesus withstands the wiles of Satan, tempting to the normal soul, and, since he is God, has not the slightest moment of weakness, the *weakness of the poem*, which leads to average versification. But the idea is subtle, because it is mandated artistically by the vision of the longer and earlier epic: Eve *is* tricked by Satan, *but Adam is not*; *knowing* that he is committing the only sin in that world, he does it out of love for Eve, as he is made to say explicitly, so that Milton can be sure Adam's reason is not taken ironically. It is out of love that he sacrifices enough to know death, and it is this same love that the Father (whose love is in His act of creating and giving life) has bequeathed indirectly to His Son, who will out of love for Adam and Eve sacrifice in turn and know death. As for the "Holy Ghost" of the bible it the same as the Urania or any of the poetic muses of *Paradise Lost*: it has no personality, and is of little significance to Milton, except as keeping to orthodoxy through appeal to emotions. The design is perfect, and Milton does effectively replace gospelJesus with himself, as was always his intent, on an intellectual plane: to eclipse the one master he couldn't without Homer's aid (*imitatio Christi*, made literal, down to becoming the Savior of Christianity from those who

He shook his Mitred locks, and stern bespake:
"How well I could have spar'd for thee, young swain,
Enough of such as for their bellies' sake
Creep and intrude and climb into the fold?"
. . . .
And when they list, their lean and flashy songs [as wild as *Hamlet*]
Grate on their scrannel Pipes of wretched straw

                                                                            Lycidas

Shakespeare himself does not write finer poetry *as language*, nor Homer).

2

Kurosawa: "Good and Evil"

Akira Kurosawa is very complex in his audiovisual manner of depicting "*philosophy*," in the sense that the word meant to Aristotle and Plato: the discovery of "Good" or "Virtue," as opposed to the "Bad" or "Evil,"— "good" and "evil" are best defined for the purposes of philosophy in an early chapter of *Leviathan*—, rather than the discovery of what is True: the only two pictures in which this good/evil complexity is not handled expertly, after Kurosawa reached full mastery with *The Hidden Fortress*, are both based on pre-existing texts: *The Bad Sleep Well* and *Ran*: perhaps, *and this may be incorrect*, if he had not had a falling out with Mifune personally, and the latter had played Hidetora, the warlord and king in *Ran*, what Kurosawa was attempting to achieve in that film, *which he rated as his best*, could have been pulled off: the extracting of pity from the audience for a character who is totally evil, but suffers in old age *after* his evil deeds have been finished.

Cinema, with the notable exception of Kurosawa, is, by nature, emotional regarding *how* the imagination *can* **understand** it, as is the case with music. Paintings, at least the greatest, tend to be purely aesthetic. Because emotion is commonplace, even the best composers and directors (*with one exception*) match at most Raphael—who is less depressing in the long run than they—, but they have yet to match the complex Michelangelo. A relative recently sent us a high-quality poster reprint of a somewhat little-known Madonna, flanked by infants Jesus and John, of Raphael (far more than the equally sublime Milton, or the biblical-themed works of da Vinci and Titian, Raphael's make the stories, figures, and situations of the New Testament (and post-biblical "saints"—usually very crazy people, if they existed) entrancing; Rembrandt with his blobs of yellowish light surrounded by a brown, and very vaguely drawn figures, of his religious paintings is quite as dreary as the Old and New Testaments themselves) that we hung today in our bedroom, replacing a view of a very and endlessly inventive-details Harlem of Jacob Lawrence, and it *shines*. We mean, the third movement of Beethoven's Ninth symphony is boring *and* depressing to the nth degree, with its "melancholy" seeming to emanate from some medieval German forest. We used to dread its imminent arrival; now we just use the remote to go to the next track, *slightly* better. *Secretly*, we prefer not only the opening song of *The Secret Akko Chan*, but the ending song as well. The problem with recorded music is, of course, that once a given work is well performed, no other version is worth hearing.

Let us say a few words about grand Americans and their chiefmost icons, as Moses is for jews and Krishna for hindus: Lincoln only made the "celebrated" Emancipation of "negroes" proclamation at the advent of victory when politically convenient, not as the *rasion d'être* of the war at the beginning. So much for the religious icons there, like the old-religions ones worldwide, in comparison to our round of heroes, to the ruthless, and pitying the weak, *moral* intellect, in *Youjinbou*, of

Kuwabatake Sanjuro, a reverse Iago (Kurosawa on his protagonist, "The idea is about rivalry on both sides, and both sides are equally bad. We all know what that is like. Here we are, weakly caught in the middle, and it is impossible to choose between evils. However, I have always wanted to stop these senseless battles of bad against bad, but we are all more or less weak—I have never been able to. And this is why the hero of this picture is different from us. He is able to stand squarely in the middle and stop the fight. And it is this—him [Kuwabatake Sanjuro]—that I thought of first. This was the beginning of the film in my mind." In 1860's America, when Lincoln reigned, Confederates thought of blacks as slaves, and the "enlightened" Yanks in the North treated them as second-class, always-segregated, citizens who could *own a shop in the black ghettos at most*: that was it: a war was fought *supposedly* over them, but truly only to keep Yanks in charge over white Southerners, who explicitly wanted to secede: banal reason (see Faulkner)—the same as Pakistanis' whose soldiers killed and raped Bengalis in the early 1970's, which we are old enough to remember, and as Pakistanis are doing *now* to Balochi separatists, who are in deep choler that their province was *raped* of its natural gas resources for decades, until they have almost none left, without any of the money going back to the province of Baluchistan—as late as May 2000 most automobiles in Pakistan were re-engineered by mechanics, so that they could run on both gasoline and cng, as it is called, concentrated natural gas, the preferred fuel there because domestically produced until they started relying on Father Putin, grandson of grandaddy "Marshal" Stalin, with buses and trucks run on messily polluting diesel: a pbs or pbs-like documentary we saw in the early or mid-1990's (a rerun?) on the Second World War: according to it, Hitler had the house in Austria where he was born razed, because rumors had started circulating that he was a half-Jew by birth: I seem to remember being convinced that with the Gestapo, Hitler would not have done so had it not been at least partly true, for he controlled the organs of propaganda in the conquered territories: he need not have worried, certainly he would not have been worried *at all*, he would have brushed it off, unless the rumor were true).

The picture of psychology, erotic in Homer (the cause of the Trojan war is erotic—a contest between three goddesses about who attracts handsome Paris most—, the cause of the fissure between Achilles and Agamemnon *equally* so—whom, of the two, must give up his slave girl to be enjoyed in bed, won as battle-loot), Shakespeare, and Stendhal—a-erotic in Kurosawa. Did people truly find an erotic reason to follow Hitler, and obey Stalin and Putin? Or Timur and Genghis Khan? Mahomet and David were *lustful* men, but were they *followed* out of sexual lust? The cause of psychology is ever in question.

Kurosawa allows creative freedom to his best characters, giving them, in *Youjinbou*, an *elasticity* reminding one of Balzac and Tolstoy at their best, though Kurosawa is much the more inventive and flourishing-styled storyteller. As for psychology, Tolstoy's consists of making observations such as (this one is in *Anna Karenina*) that a person can sit for hours with one leg folded on the knee of the other for hours, but just tell him or her once to do so, and it will seem unbearably irksome: observations that are both trivial nor *always* true. Tibetan Buddhist monks, many of whom live currently in India, remain frozen for hours in the same posture, because of force of will. And the *Encyclopædia Britannica* used to call him in the introduction to their article on him, "one of the greatest writers of the world," before they became more modish and changed this to "a master of realistic fiction, and one of the world's greatest novelists," merely.

In *Seven Samurai*, Kurosawa starts as a didactic narrative artist, always seeking to make a point, until the scene when Shimura Takashi, who plays the lead of the six and a half samurai, appears for the first time, getting his head shaved to look like a Buddhist priest, so that he can corner a thief who has taken a child hostage: from thence characters take over, and obvious moralizing is diminished, and the film begins to be only a few steps below *Youjinbou*. (Those who have not read much of the later Henry James, or Conrad, are highly impressed by *Rashomon*: psychological perspectives given from different characters' points of view.) The heroics of *The Hidden Fortress* are parodies, and the triumph of the film is not such much the dialogue lines of the two peasants, but the direction of the actors who portray them.

One of the most unfortunate facts about international-level art is that Kurosawa mistook himself for a "dark" artist of the sort as are Melville and Faulkner and Dostoevsky (whose *The Idiot* he adapted without improving it, nor falling short of it): when, as the reader, who has seen *The Hidden Fortress* and *Youjinbou* hundreds of times, will surely have noted, with all the dangers and deaths that are depicted in them, they are as comic as *Much Ado About Nothing* and *The Charterhouse of Parma*. At his best, he was a hugely funny comic artist, much more amusing than sentimental Dickens or sentimental Chaplin. But all those failures, *The Idiot*, *Ikiru*, *The Lower Depths*, *Cobweb Castle* (also known as *Throne of Blood*), *The Bad Sleep Well*, they were paid off by the nearly *ten-year attention* Kurosawa gave in his (fortunately, temporary) enforced retirement during the 1970's **to** *Kagemusha*, a masterly exposition of the *charisma of evil*—the double, played by Nakadai, who also plays the massively murderous warlord Shingen, *only* agrees to perform that role of shadow warrior or double because he is deeply moved by the "*attractive nature*" of the crass and hugely criminal actuality of the warlord Shingen (who is portrayed, with the usual Kurosawian subtlety, as a *refined* man), not because he is afraid of being *brutally* executed. He braves death for the sake of Shingen, literally so, at the end of the picture.

(We used to admire the highly artistic use of horses, their beauty and muscles and stretch, by Tarkovsky in *The Passion According to Andrei*—but it is clear to us today that he was merely imitating Kurosawa, who is the only filmmaker to have successfully done so. This fact became clear when we looked again at the horse scene in Tarkovsky's subsequent work, in color, *Solaris*, which is tremulously weak: this is because Kurosawa had not yet made a color film (which has a different aesthetics from a black-and-white film's) with horses as artistically crucial, and Kurosawa was to do so first in *Kagemusha*, almost a decade after *Solaris*, Kurosawa's favorite Tarkovsky film. In fact, Kurosawa once said about him, "He is a poet, I am not." A similar occurrence happened in painting. Rubens was (and will probably remain forever) the greatest painter of horses in northeastsouthwest art, and was imitated coarsely by Delacroix, along with Picasso, the most overrated painter.)

Melville's best novellas also convey an a-erotic view of psychology (Faulkner's best novels suggest an erotic one), but then—see the courtesy address DEDICATION where he greets his dedicatee,

DEDICATED
TO
JACK CHASE
ENGLISHMAN

Wherever that great heart may now be
Here on Earth or harbored in Paradise

Captain of the Maintop
in the year 1843
in the U.S. Frigate
United States

, beginning *Billy Budd*—Melville believed *with certainty* in a Christian afterlife of *sexless angels* ever hymning the praise of the LORD.

Kurosawa *may* have been as orthodox as Melville, not about Christo-fancies but about Buddoholistic ones: the song at the peasants' fire festival in *The Hidden Fortress* is repeated by Princess Yuki one night before her scheduled execution, and the hymn that the quite historical warlord, Oda Nobunaga, in *Kagemusha*, is made to recite, in mourning the death of his deadly film enemy, Shingen, immediately after Nobunaga has learned of Shingen's funeral—both Princess Yuki and Lord Nobunaga sing of life disappearing into the dark, life like an insect's, and "Life is but a dream" (also the idea behind Calderón's most famous play's dream), that Rokurota's and Princess Yuki's ultimate savior, and not one of the three villains of the picture's title, Tadokoro Hiyoe, the rival general to villain Rokurota, also embraces, during his "treachery" to his stupid warlord of the Yamana clan's conquest cause. Notions of Japanese Buddhism?

Of course, no one with the sense of humor manifest in *The Hidden Fortress*, or, to call it by its full title, *The Three Villains of the Hidden Fortress*, could have been a sincere Buddhist. Probably the funniest (not wittiest) scene in all of art is that of Matashichi and Tahei squabbling after having dug a huge hole in front of that hidden fortress, so huge that it cannot be called merely a hole (almost a trench), that scene ending with their running off to the stream where they both now suspect (correctly, as it turns out) the gold pieces are hidden. One cannot describe the funny, so I will quote from Shakespeare in the one sequence where he, and only he, rivals Kurosawa in comedy,

MALVOLIO Calling my officers about me, in my branched velvet gown, having come from a daybed where I have left Olivia sleeping—

TOBY, aside Fire and brimstone!

FABIAN, aside O, peace, peace!

MALVOLIO And then to have the humor of state; and after a demure travel of regard, telling them I know my place, as I would they should do theirs, to ask for my kinsman Toby—

TOBY, aside Bolts and shackles!

FABIAN, aside O, peace, peace, peace! Now, now.

MALVOLIO Seven of my people, with an obedient start, make out for him. I frown the while, and perchance wind up my watch, or play with my—some rich jewel. Toby approaches; curtsies there to me—

TOBY, aside Shall this fellow live?

FABIAN, aside Though our silence be drawn from us with cars, yet peace!

MALVOLIO I extend my hand to him thus, quenching my familiar smile with an austere regard of control—

TOBY, aside And does not Toby take you a blow o' the lips then?

MALVOLIO Saying, "Cousin Toby, my fortunes, having cast me on your niece, give me this prerogative of speech—"

TOBY, aside What, what?

MALVOLIO "You must amend your drunkenness."

TOBY, aside Out, scab!

FABIAN, aside Nay, patience, or we break the sinews of our plot!

MALVOLIO "Besides, you waste the treasure of your time with a foolish knight—"

ANDREW, aside That's me, I warrant you.

MALVOLIO "One Sir Andrew."
ANDREW, aside I knew 'twas I, for many do call me
fool.

Kurosawa's idea of battle of evils carries over into
Youjinbou's first half, until the "intermission" break before
the son-for-ownedwoman exchange takes place. After it,
the hero does side with one small group of people, and
this would have been a deadly flaw, as Hawks' most
famous Western is in the second third of the unfolding of
its plot, when the "drunk" is making attemps to abjure
drinks: We prefer the dialogue exchange in *Youjinbou*:

Sanjuro. I have no intention of beating and slitting all of
them myself.
The restaurant owner. Then what do you intend to do?
Sanjuro. Sakéda. While drinking saké (rice-wine; liquor), to
think deeply.

Had it not been for the superb, Miltonic design of
Sanjuro's breaking off from his character (after all, he is
never moved to help the abducted and sold women in the
gambler honcho's brothel), only to complete his original
intention of killing all gamblers left in town, and thus
baptizing and cleansing it, *Youjinbou* would have been an
artistic disaster in its second half.

Sanjuro in *Youjinbou* can feel only disgust faced with
brothel women dancing to music, when he is
"entertained" so, after he has brought the two murderers
of a nearby town's magistrate to one of the evil sides of

the two evil sides, Seibei's, to trap the *other* gambler chief, Ushitora—there is not the slightest *arousal*.

One of the *two* main themes of Kurosawa's *Kagemusha*, the one that has been outlined, ends with the Noh performance scene in it, when the "lookalike" has acknowledged his *defeat before the charisma of evil*; the rest of the film, except for the last battle scene that returns to it, is occupied with the theme of *acting*, the "double" acting *as* the real Shingen, the actor working as if he or she is the character portrayed, while suffering a loss of his own personality as a result—this is of considerable import to Kurosawa as the supreme director of actors in cinema. Shakespeare's theme of "playing" in *Hamlet* does not take into consideration the cinematic "close-up" invented by the notorious D.W. Griffith, because close-ups did not exist (for Richard Burbage playing King Lear) in all-male acting on stage, as it existed in Shakespeare's time.

3

Homer and God

Look at *The Iliad* (for the following reason alone we would claim that *The Odyssey* is by a different oral composer, an ur-*Aeneid*): its central character(s) is neither Achilles, the focal point of the action of the plot, nor Agamemnon, his foe among Achaeans, nor Hector, the Trojan he slays as the climactic act of the poem, but Zeus, who seems *to bend to* other gods and goddesses, and especially to what the *Fates are spinning*, but, as Zeus once tells the other Olympians, remember that when you all, all together, conspired against me, and I bound all of you together and suspended you in the air, you all together; I am that much stronger than all of you combined: there is nothing you can do against what I wish

The cleverest idea of a God:

This much has always and already been remarked of Homer (I can include only *The Iliad* here—Caroline Alexander's recent translation into English, purportedly and palpably, when compared to the slack but presumably accurate crib of the Loeb-Harvard transposition of this poem, linear *and* interlinear conversion for the *first* time, makes it clear to someone who only reads *The Iliad* in our language something close to what it will be as in classical Greek—, as there *is* no, and, to known knowledge, never has been, a translation, properly speaking (so I do not understand the fuss over it when not read in the original) of *The Odyssey*, into English, at least)), that he remains uniformly detached from the subject of his work in a manner that is called epic because it began with him.

This is much, but it is not enough, perhaps. Of others, later, this may be said also. But is this what Homer intended, to write a massive oral performance entertainment for the ancient crowds to pass innocent evenings?

Within a little or more I have read of Homer scholarship I see little comprehension of what critics have seen him to be attempting to do, aside from telling with inimitable force, until the verses of Shakespeare, the story of Troy and Helen.

Did he wish to be judged so?

I am not sure.

What I do note is that in the central passage in Book Two where Odysseus addresses the Argives to continue their so far thankless drive to sack Troy, Zeus-fate-humans are brought together to form a tripartite scheme, (allow me the long quotation)

For this we know well in our minds—you are all
witnesses, you whom the fates of death have not carried off,
only yesterday, as it seems—when the Achaean ships in Aulis
were gathered bearing evil for Priam and Troy,
and we around a spring and about the sacred altars

performed perfect sacrificial hecatombs for the immortals,
beneath a lovely plane tree, from where bright water flowed;
and there appeared a momentous portent; a snake, its back mottled blood-red,
a thing of dread that the Olympian himself dispatched into the light,
darting from beneath the altar sped toward the plane tree—
where a sparrow's nestlings were, innocent young,
on the tip-top branch, cowering beneath the leaves,
eight of them, and the mother made nine, who gave them life.
There it devoured them as they cheeped piteously,
the mother fluttering around, crying for her beloved children.
Then, having coiled itself up, it seized her by the wing as she cried about.
. . . .
In this way, then, the terrible portent of the gods broke into our hecatombs."
Thereupon Calchas spoke at once, prophesying:
"Why are you become silent, O long-haired Achaeans?
Zeus, all devising, brought to light this great omen for us,
late arriving, late to be fulfilled, and the fame of which will never die.
As this thing devoured the sparrow's young and the sparrow herself—
eight they were, but the mother made nine, who gave them life

                              [the pathos subtly being built for Homer's
overall theme in the poem]—
so for as many years we shall wage battle here,
and in the tenth we shall take the city of wide ways."

                                                         (ll. 301-329)

This passage is not merely a matter of describing, epically and vividly, ancient realities of myth, supposedly, according to Oxford and Harvard Universities with the use of "oral formulae," that most hideous and fake (scholarly, academic, entombed) invention in the whole history of literary commentary, that are deliberately left vague as to whether the persona of the poet believes in them or not; the thesis about Homer for millennia, it would seem.

   In that pathos and the pitiless waging of battle is the will of Zeus, and the question of whether it can be trusted or not, the all-devising son of Time's *promises*. This is the central theme, and Homer's attitude towards it is not that of a Greek or Persian, Chinese or Egyptian, of this or that time—it is of a human confronting fate more deviously than Shakespeare in *Macbeth* or Conrad in *Lord Jim* or Nabokov in *Lolita*.

   How? By comparing and juxtaposing the beginning and end of the poem, in which Homer structures and encapsulates his sense of brutal response to the inimicality, only potential (so that it is markedly different from Melville's certainty of it in his pre-mature *Moby-Dick*, and from Camus's ultimately comforting—which is why *The Stranger* is so much more popular than Sartre's forgotten and forgettable *Nausea—certainty*   of its benignity, also, "And I, too, felt ready to start life all over again. It was as if that great rush of anger had washed me clean, emptied me of hope, and, gazing up at the dark sky spangled with its signs and stars, for the first time, the first, I laid my heart open to the benign indifference of the universe."), of what may be called the seduction of order within what is really only portentous disorder, with a sense of purposed and intellectual form not seen again until at least Joyce and Proust (though Dante without Homer's aid, and Milton, with, also came close as constructers, but not thinkers). The poem begins with Zeus and his favors,

Wrath—sing, goddess, of the ruinous wrath of Peleus'
son Achilles
that inflicted woes without number upon the Achaeans,
hurled forth to Hades many strong souls of warriors
and rendered their bodies prey for the dogs,
for all birds, and the will of Zeus was accomplished.

And of what character is this will of Zeus that carries the day, this is what we get from the deeply ironic concluding lines of the poem, each word and phrase counting ("nurtured"),

And taking the bones [of Hector] they placed them in a
golden box,
after covering them round with soft purple cloth;
swiftly they placed these in a hollowed grave, and covered
it from above with great stones set together.

Lightly they heaped up the burial ground—lookouts were set all round,
lest the strong-greaved Achaeans should attack before—
and when they had piled up the mound they started back.
Then having come together they duly gave a glorious feast
in the house of Priam, king nurtured by Zeus.
Thus they tended to the funeral of Hector, breaker of horses.

The weariless tragic mode has not been handled since as complexly (the fourteenth-century Chinese novel, Luo Guanzhoung's *The Three Kingdoms* (the *Mahabharata* of China) as it is known in one English version, begins and ends with the idea of empires splitting and coalescing over time unendingly, and in the middle interchangeable characters and actions are inserted, as in *One Hundred Years of Solitude*, but end up being simple illustrations of that perhaps true, but also for the purposes of art, trite idea: the opposite of Homer who is not interested in writing a simple work such as intended by the later born Chinese and Colombian) or with as much delicacy teleological, unless it be in certain paintings of Titian, such as, among others, one of the versions of *Tarquin and Lucretia* or those of Jesus being assailed near the steps, or *The Death of Actaeon*, depicting his being killed by Artemis.

In such Titian paintings there in contrast a metaphysical fear of the psychological found in human imagination.

4

Stendhal and Shakespeare: Psychology

Literature at its best, Shakespeare and Stendhal, is intellectual and aesthetic at the same time.

We observe that perhaps Shakespeare's greatest psychological insight is, with obvious exceptions of *lonely* derangements of the brain, as in mass "shooters" one knows from Sweden or America in recent years, etc., that *the deepest murderous instincts derive from the nature of the relationships between men and women*: Claudius, the two sisters of Cordelia, Iago (he can bring himself to tell himself that he hates Othello because he has heard the rumor, which, whether true or not, he thinks, since he doesn't know, he will believe, that the "thick lips" performed Iago's office in bed with Emilia, but even he says *only* "perhaps" because he lusts after Othello's "fair" wife), Macbeth (being egged on to kill Duncan by a woman to whom Shakespeare gives a personality and a style of language that make her seem to be Macbeth's *stern* aunt or grandmother: you can't imagine them sleeping together comfortably lodged in the same bed, though she says— Shakespeare obviously making up for the "mistake" that he knows somebody on his own level will note— somewhat late in the play that she has suckled a child in the past): between Hitler and Braun, between Nero and his mother: in other cases in history the facts of the past have *simply not been revealed to posterity*. They *have* for "King" David and "Prophet" Muhammad (i.e., Mahomet), *founders*, respectively, of *judaism* (it was under David, and during David's reign, that the bible began to be composed as God's dictation to the never-existed Moses) and *islam*, two cancerous *diseases* now each fighting it out, each with the other, in a trashy remake of *Youjinbou*—and the forerunner, David, as supposed ancestor, of poor little cross-fated "Christ."

This is little Darwin raised to the level of knowledge.

Stendhal writes,

from *The Red and the Black*,

His moral uneasiness, in Mathilde's presence, was all the more marked, in that he inspired in her at that moment the most extraordinary and insensate passion. She could speak of nothing, but the strange sacrifices which she was anxious to make to save his life.

Carried away by the sentiment of which she was proud and which completely overbore her pride, she would have liked not to allow a moment of her life to pass that was not filled with some extraordinary action. The strangest of actions, the most perilous to her herself, formed the theme of her long conversations with Julien. His gaolers, well rewarded, allowed her to have her way in the prison. Mathilde's ideas were not confined to the sacrifice of her reputation; it mattered nothing to her though she made her condition known to the whole of society. To fling herself on her knees to crave pardon for Julien, in front of the King's carriage as it came by at a gallop, to attract the royal attention, at the risk of a thousand deaths, was one of the tamest fancies of this exalted and courageous imagination. Through her friends, who held posts at court, she could count upon being admitted to the reserved parts of the park of Saint-Cloud.

Julien felt himself to be hardly worthy of such devotion, to tell the truth he was tired of heroism.

And some pages later, Julien's thoughts in prison,

'There is no such thing as *natural law*: the expression is merely a hoary piece of stupidity well worthy of the Advocate-General who hunted me down the other day, and whose ancestor was made rich by one of Louis XIV's confiscations. There is no *law*, save when there is a statute to prevent one from doing something, on pain of punishment. Before the statute, there was nothing *natural* save the strength of the lion, or the wants of the creature who suffers through hunger, or cold; in a word, *necessity*. No, the men we honour are merely rascals who have had the good fortune not to be caught red-handed. The accusers whom society sets at my heels have been made rich by a scandalous injustice…..'

This philosophy might be true, but it was of a nature to make a man long for death….

'A hunter fires his gun in a forest, his quarry falls, he runs forward to seize it. His boot strikes an anthill two feet high, destroys the habitation of the ants, scatters the ants and their eggs to the four winds … The most philosophical among the ants will never understand that black, enormous, fearful body—the hunter's boot which all of a sudden has burst into their dwelling with incredible speed, preceded by a terrifying noise, accompanied by a flash of reddish flame …

So it is with death, life, eternity, things that would be quite simple to anyone who had organs vast enough to conceive them …

An ephemeral fly is born at nine o'clock in the morning on one of the longs days of summer, to die at five o'clock in the afternoon; how should it understand the word night?

Give it five more hours of existence, it sees and understands what night is.'

And Stendhal implies there is no escape. Only a few pages earlier,

'… need we part?' [Mme de Rênal] said, with a smile.

'I take back my word,' cried Julien, springing to his feet; 'I shall not appeal from the sentence of death, if by poison, knife, pistol, charcoal or any other means whatsoever, you seek to put an end to, or to endanger your life.'

'If we were to die at once?' she asked him at length.

'Who knows what we shall find in our next life?' replied Julien; 'torments, perhaps, perhaps nothing at all. Can we not spend two months together in a delicious manner? Two months, that is ever so many days. Never shall I have been so happy.'

(in one place, we cannot remember where, even Stendhal (he admired the unfunny *Don Quixote* (Stendhal was a great psychologist/philosopher and the supreme novelist, but a poor critic: he admired *De l'esprit*, he preferred

Correggio to Raphael, the composer Cimarosa to Beethoven, and thought Dante was nearly as sublime as Shakespeare)—the novel *seems to be* on the level of the best of Stendhal, Dostoevsky, Tolstoy, and Joyce because Don Quixote, an artistically *very dead* character, seems to embody a search for ultimate ideals, beauty, truth, heroism, in parodic form, but Sancho, who saves the novel, as Jesus saves humanity, is an artistically very greatly conceived but even more greatly *executed* character—even more inspired than Fielding's Parson Adams—, and the result, for *most* sensitive readers is that the novel *seems to be a powerfully* **realistic** *vision of human* **ideals**: *this* result is an *illusion* that does not recognize its *psychological evolution*, but is so universally felt by readers, that *Don Quixote* seems larger and more *mature* than Dickens, Fielding, Austen, Melville, Faulkner, Proust, Kafka, Mann, Chekhov, Balzac, Molière, even Stendhal, and on the level of the two Russians, etc.) adds in mentioning the date April 23, 1616 as that of Shakespeare's death, as, otherwise, mediocrities always do, that died on that day, too, Cervantes, who was barely one step better than P. G. Wodehouse, that utterly boring and flat British writer, and fan of the New York Mets, a baseball team: Cervantes, who made the *fatal* mistake, *artistically*, merely to appear to be a pious man—he spent his last days sheltered by a monastery, we believe, as did Calderón, too, *if we remember correctly*—, of having Don Quixote admit on his deathbed that *he invented his madness*, and knew all along he was pretending: no one *forced* Cervantes' hand in writing this: the first part of the novel, published ten years earlier, had been accepted enthusiastically by rabble and king alike; we first read his famous novel at sixteen, in six days, and found it utterly barren in interest, and have not been able to reread even ten pages of it again without being consumed "by yawns": fellow "renegade," Mr. Rushdie—he publicly would define himself as a "non-practising Muslim" until he became *internationally famous*, **since when** he has defined himself fashionably as an "atheist" (!) to *curry* favor with London and New York "critics"—, finds it so amusing that he imitated it for six or seven hundred *ghastly* pages a few years ago: Mr. Rushdie has moved from England to New York, as Mr. John Lennon did earlier, both knowing which is the more *lucrative* **market**: "Money, money, money," "it's so funny," as the Swedish pop group ABBA sang in the 1970's)

—compare Julien's thoughts to Einstein's (high-speed "*approaching* the speed of light") foolish line, "Nature speaks the language of mathematics." Actually, it speaks in French, and in English (Shakespeare). What a femininely square mind that Einstein possessed. "Nature speaks the language of mathematics," indeed! Only physicists, chemists, engineers, and economists do. This *profound* statement, which Einstein should have said is an idea he stole from Newton, surely would have been of a lot of use to Charles Darwin! Darwin hit upon a truth far more pertinent: that it is *all* the "survival of the fittest": to which we should add the term of "chance," for dinosaurs were the fittest until an asteroid hit earth: then, by *chance*, they became the least fit, and died *en masse*, unlike cockroaches. The actual formula is: "survival of the luckiest.")

Compare Julien's thoughts in the cell, again, to this, which hardly gets to the heart o' the matter; just empty, *conventional* Christian *double-talk*, what it and all other religions are built of, lying,

Hamlet. Now might I do it pat, now 'a is praying.
And now I'll do it. And so 'a goes to heaven.
And so I am revenged. That would be scanned.

Moreover, we must remember that Hamlet here is *not* Shakespeare, the latter of whom is just pointing out the price of religious prankery. Harold Bloom, in his senile years, those of this century, proclaimed that Hamlet is *more intelligent than Shakespeare*. A character may be wittier or more charismatic than his creator, but never more intelligent. Nabokov got to the heart of this matter in responding to an interviewer's question about Van in *Ada* (I paraphrase from memory from his *Strong Opinions*), "The more intelligent a character, the more he resembles his author." And unfortunately, for the writers of English-language commentaries on Shakespeare, Hamlet and Falstaff, who are often if not usually designated as the most interesting or "greatest" or "most intelligent" of his innumerable great characters (for example, in *Ulysses*, Hamlet is the one debated upon in the library scene with Stephen holding forth on the Prince, is also the passage,

—She lies laid out in stark stiffness in that secondbest bed, the mobled queen, even though you prove that a bed in those days was as rare as a motorcar is now and that its carvings were the wonder of seven parishes. In old age she takes up with gospellers (one stayed with her at New Place and drank a quart of sack the town council paid for but in which bed he slept it skills not to ask) and heard she had a soul. She read or had read to her his chapbooks preferring them to the *Merry Wives* and, loosing her nightly waters on the jordan, she thought over *Hooks and Eyes for Believers' Breeches* and *The most Spiritual Snuffbox to Make the Most Devout Souls Sneeze*. Venus has twisted her lips in prayer. Agenbite of inwit: remorse of conscience. It is an age of exhausted whoredom groping for its god.

—History shows that to be true, *inquit Eglintonus Chronololologos*. The ages succeed one another. But we have it on high authority that a man's worst enemies shall be those of his own house and family. I feel that Russell is right. What do we care for his wife or father? I should say that only family poets have family lives. Falstaff was not a family man. I feel that the fat knight is his supreme creation.

)

, unfortunately for these John Eglinton's of history, the most intelligent character created, consciously so, it seems, by Shakespeare, was Iago.

'

5

The Ten

But let it be so, if it were so, we have not been invited yet to proffer our own "best of all" itemized balance default by the internet booksandwriters dot org connected loosely and hazily perhaps to a merchant retailer that has sent out invitations to the popular masters of our métier. We of course did try other methods, especially the tricky one of taking advantage of our friendship with the brother of its editor's wife, who like us belongs to the lowly unionized portion of the otherwise haute couture American Authors' Guild, to suggest a written request. We meanwhile give out our best books of all time (our enumeration compares as apples do watermelons with Volodya's five, ferreted into a corner of his commentary to Pushkin's poem, where he compares Pushkin's ending with the endings (in reverse order) of *Hamlet*, *Madame Bovary*, *Ulysses*, and *Anna Karenin* [*sic*]. Reversed or not?) as do recorded at that site veterans such as Mr. Coover and Mr. Barnes all the way to beautiful younglings. We now make our top ten list, with brief comments, if necessary.

1. The Tragedy of Othello, the Moor of Venice

It could have been called *The Comedy of Iago, the Ancient of Venice* by its author, and have been *as* correct. Right from when Othello and Iago are first seen together,

IAGO
Though in the trade of war I have slain men,
Yet do I hold it very stuff o' th' conscience
To do no contriv'd murder: I lack iniquity
Sometimes to do me service: nine or ten times
I had thought t' have yerk'd him here under the ribs.
OTHELLO
'Tis better as it is.

, to the full-blown blackness of *laughter* by its fourth "act,"

OTHELLO
Ay, you did wish that I would make her turn.
Sir, she can turn, and turn, and yet go on,
And turn again. And she can weep, sir, weep.
And she's obedient, as you say, obedient.
Very obedient.—Proceed you in your tears.—
Concerning this, sir—O, well-painted passion!—
I am commanded home.—Get you away.
I'll send for you anon.—Sir, I obey the mandate
And will return to Venice.—Hence, avaunt!
[*Exit Desdemona*]
Cassio shall have my place. And, sir, tonight
I do entreat that we may sup together.
You are welcome, sir, to Cyprus. Goats and
monkeys!
[*Exit Othello*].
LODOVICO
Is this the noble Moor, whom our full senate
Call all in all sufficient? Is this the nature
Whom passion could not shake, whose solid virtue

The shot of accident nor dart of chance
Could neither graze nor pierce?
IAGO   He is much
changed.
LODOVICO
Are his wits safe? Is he not light of brain?
IAGO
He's that he is. I may not breathe my censure
What he might be. If what he might he is not,
I would to heaven he were.
LODOVICO   What? Strike his wife?
IAGO
'Faith, that was not so well. Yet would I knew
That stroke would prove the worst.
LODOVICO   Is it his use?
Or did the letters work upon his blood
And new-create this fault?
IAGO   Alas, alas!
It is not honesty in me to speak
What I have seen and known. You shall observe him,
And his own courses will denote him so
That I may save my speech. Do but go after
And mark how he continues.
LODOVICO
I am sorry that I am deceived in him.
[*Exeunt*]

2. *Julius Caesar*

In the following scene, Shakespeare on *the rule of the people,
by the people, and for the people*. How he imagined he may be

treated by *the people*, that is, as badly as by queen or king of England, were he to tell *them* his true sentiments.

Act III, scene iii, *Julius Caesar*,

CINNA
I dreamt tonight that I did feast with Caesar,
And things unluckily charge my fantasy.
I have no will to wander forth of doors,
Yet something leads me forth.
FIRST PLEBEIAN What is your name?
SECOND PLEBEIAN Whither are you going?
THIRD PLEBEIAN Where do you dwell?
FOURTH PLEBEIAN Are you a married man or a bachelor?
SECOND PLEBEIAN Answer every man directly.
FIRST PLEBEIAN Ay, and briefly.
FOURTH PLEBEIAN Ay, and wisely.
THIRD PLEBEIAN Ay, and truly, you were best.
CINNA What is my name? Whither am I going? Where do I dwell? Am I a married man or a bachelor? Then to answer every man directly and briefly, wisely and truly: wisely I say, I am a bachelor.
SECOND PLEBEIAN That's as much as to say they are fools that marry. You'll bear me a bang for that, I fear. Proceed directly.
CINNA Directly, I am going to Caesar's funeral.
FIRST PLEBEIAN As a friend or an enemy?
CINNA As a friend.
SECOND PLEBEIAN That matter is answered directly.

FOURTH PLEBEIAN For your dwelling—briefly.
CINNA Briefly, I dwell by the Capitol.
THIRD PLEBEIAN Your name, sir, truly.
CINNA Truly, my name is Cinna.
FIRST PLEBEIAN Tear him to pieces! He's a conspirator.
CINNA I am Cinna the poet, I am Cinna the poet!
FOURTH PLEBEIAN Tear him for his bad verses, tear him for his bad verses!
CINNA I am not Cinna the conspirator.
FOURTH PLEBEIAN It is no matter. His name's Cinna. Pluck but his name out of his heart, and turn him going.
THIRD PLEBEIAN Tear him, tear him! Come, brands, ho! Firebrands! To Brutus', to Cassius', burn all! Some to Decius' house, and some to Casca's, some to Ligarius'. Away, go!

All the Plebeians exit, carrying off Cinna.

—a much finer play, *Julius Caesar* (though Shakespeare has no interest in the dictator: he gives Caesar fine sounding lines that are shallow and callow) than is *Hamlet* (*Julius Caesar* is much more sophisticated politically—which Shakespeare could not be in the English-history plays, for fear of being treated as Cinna the poet is, by Elizabeth I and James I—, and much less muddleheaded metaphysically, than the play about the Prince and his father), of which it has long supposed, by university professors and high school teachers, to be an understudy: and not greater for the reason Nietzsche gives in his "*In*

Praise of Shakespeare"—The Gay Science).

3. *The Red and the Black*

As extraordinary in its deep lyricism,

(Translated by C.K. Scott Moncrieff, revised by Ann Jefferson, *still not good enough!*)

"

Outside the door were gathered on their knees four and twenty girls, belonging to the most distinguished families of Verrières. Before opening the door, the Bishop sank on his knees in the midst of these girls, who were all pretty. While he was praying aloud, it seemed as though they could not sufficiently admire his fine lace, his charm, his young and pleasant face. The spectacle made our hero lose all that remained of his reason. At that moment, he would have fought for the Inquisition, and in earnest. Suddenly the door flew open. The little chapel seemed to be ablaze with light....

Presently the King arrived....

His Majesty flung himself rather than knelt down on the priedieu faldstool. It was then that Julien, pressed against the gilded door, caught sight, beneath a girl's bare arm, of the charming statue of St. Clement. It was hidden beneath the altar, in the garb of a young Roman soldier. He had in his throat a large wound from which the blood seemed to be flowing. The artist had surpassed himself; the eyes, dying but full of grace, were half closed. A budding moustache adorned the charming mouth, which being slightly open had the effect of being still engaged in prayer. At the sight of this statue, the girl nearest to Julien wept hot tears; one of her tears fell upon Julien's hand."

(what are *all* of Proust and Chateaubriand and Hugo—or, Racine, Molière, and Baudelaire—, compared to *this*?) (… I have *just* understood, I thought then, that all dispraise of not Stendhal, but of this novel of Stendhal *in particular*, arises from *envy* and *fear*: Sainte-Beuve, Hugo, Balzac, Flaubert, Nabokov,—Auerbach (in Auerbach's chapter 18 on *The Red* in the scholarly classic, *Mimesis* (1953), "The characters, attitudes, and relationships of the dramatis personae [in *The Red and the Black*], then, are very closely connected with contemporary historical circumstances; contemporary political and social conditions are woven into the action in a manner more detailed and more real than had been exhibited in any previous novel, and indeed in any work of literary art except those expressly purporting to be politico-satirical tracts. So logically and systematically to situate the tragically conceived life of a man of low social position (as here that of Julian Sorel) and within the most concrete kind of contemporary history and to develop it therefrom—this is an entirely new and highly significant phenomenon. The other circles in which Julien Sorel moves—his father's family, the house of the mayor of Verrières, M. de Rênal, the seminary of Besançon—are sociologically defined in conformity with the historical moment with the same penetration as in the La Mole household, and none of the minor characters—the old priest Chélan, for example, or the director of the *dépôt de mendicité*, Valenod—would be conceivable outside the particular historical situation of the Restoration period, in the manner in which they are set before us. The same laying of a contemporary foundation for events is to be found in Stendhal's other novels—still incomplete and too narrowly circumscribed in *Armance*, but fully developed in the *Chartreuse de Parme* (which, however, since its setting is a place not yet greatly affected by modern development, sometimes gives the effect of being a historical novel), as also in *Lucien Leuwen*, a novel of the Louis-Philippe period, which Stendhal left unfinished. In the latter, indeed, in the form in which it has come down to us, the element of current history and politics is too heavily emphasized: it is not always wholly integrated into the course of the action and is set forth in far too great detail in proportion to the principal theme; but perhaps in a final revision Stendhal would have achieved an organic articulation of the whole. Finally, his autobiographical works, despite the capricious and erratic "egotism" of their style and manner, are likewise far more closely, essentially, and concretely connected with the politics, sociology, and economics of the period than are, for example, the corresponding works of Rousseau or Goethe; one feels that the great events of contemporary history affected Stendhal much more directly than they did the other two; Rousseau did not live to see them, and Goethe had managed to keep aloof from them…. **[So far Auerbach has written in the manner of an able scholar.]**

"We may ask ourselves how it came to be that modern consciousness of reality began to find literary form for the first time precisely in Henri Beyle of Grenoble. Beyle-

Stendhal was a man of keen intelligence, quick and alive, mentally independent and courageous, but not quite a great figure. His ideas are often forceful and inspired, but they are erratic, arbitrarily advanced, and, despite all their show of boldness, lacking in inward certainty and continuity,…" **(that is to say, Stendhal did not have the** *urbanity* **of scholars like Auerbach, who write smoothly and evenly, and have "***balanced***" minds: that is all: envy** *and* **fear]**, Harold Bloom (for whom Macbeth, the tyrant, is "doom-eager" but Julien, not a king, is merely a stunted self-destructor: "doom-eager" sounds *grand*, while the "*sparamagos*" (a word defined by dictionary dot com as "the tearing to pieces of a live victim, as a bull or calf, by a band of bacchantes in a Dionysian orgy") for Julien seems a *diminutive*), "Julien Sorel, in *The Red and the Black*, pursues his suicidal and more or less heroic erotic career as a Napoleonic clone bound to undergo a *sparamagos* in the Restoration." What is the *source* of the envy for Bloom, who used to sleep *passionlessly* with many of his female *students*? The cause of this envy, and resulting fear because of wounded vanity, is stated by Bloom a paragraph above the one just quoted, from his *How to Read and Why* (2000), "If Stendhal had a passion, beyond his unfulfilled lust for certain women who had evaded him, it was for Napoleonic idealism." Now, Stendhal ("more or less heroic erotic career" of Julien, Stendhal's "lust" for "certain women"), may not have slept with *all* the women he loved—though he slept with quite a large percentage of them—, but *lived* through *les grande passions* **many** times in his life; whereas Bloom had wretched little Woodyallenish affairs with women younger than he, on whom he could pass Yahweh-like academic judgements by "giving" them "low grades" in prestigious Yale literature classes), Robert M. Adams, etc., etc. It is both equally, *envy*, that Stendhal can do things better than "you" can, and *fear*, that he attacks what "you love." Here is Nabokov, from his commentary to his translation of Pushkin's *Eugene Onegin*, note to line 13 of stanza XXXVIII of chapter seven of that "novel in verse": "In Pisenski's *A Thousand Souls,* a kind of Russian *Le Rouge et le Noir*, and on the same level of paltry literary style, there is…" Where in the whole of the overwritten *Lolita* and *Ada*, Nabokov's most "lyrical" novels, is there a passage as "literary styled," in good taste, as the one quoted above from *The Red and the Black*? So, it is envy. Where does the envy rise from? From fear. In a section in the second Book of *The Red and the Black* where Julien speaks to a Russian nobleman in Paris, hitting Nabokov's vanity about his doomed homeland hard: in fact Nabokov returns to that one theme of Russia in Stendhal's novel two or three times of the few occasions in which he refers to it in the commentary: Nabokov writes, (I shall not translate Stendhal's French here, as Nabokov does not, that great, great translator and writer),

Nabokov's note to line 7 of stanza XVII of the first chapter of Pushkin's poem. The words in the poem commented upon are translated by Nabokov as "enchanting actresses." Here is Nabokov,

"Cf. Stendhal, *Le Rouge et le Noir* (1831), ch. 24:

'Ah ça, mon cher [dit le prince Korasoff à Julien Sorel] … series-vous amoreux de quelque petite actrice?" Les Russes copient le mœurs françaises, mais toujours à cinquante ans de distance. Il en sont maintenant [in 1830] au siècle de Louis XV.'

So are Stendhal's Russians of 1830's; they belong to the eighteenth-century literary type of traveling Muscovites." *When Pushkin himself is writing in the eighteenth-century mode of novels* such as Frances Burney's, done much better in the nineteenth century when the Russian poet is so doing, by Austen in England a decade and a half before *Eugene Onegin.* This fool, Nabokov, does not even realize that *Eugene Onegin* is a pre-Walter Scott novel! Why? Because he fears the accuracy of Stendhal on Stendhal's contemporary Russians, the aspersion on Russian culture of *Pushkin's* time, and, therefore, on Pushkin: in fact Pushkin, *very* famous *within* Russia, as much as Tolstoy was to be in the future, read *The Red and the Black*, as Pushkin noted in a letter, and praised a Goethe novel or some trash like that more; and never made Stendhal known in Russia through Pushkin's very publicized career; and neither did Goethe in German states and principalities, Goethe, that total idiot with his sickening German-sentimental heroines in poems and novels, after reading *The Red and the Black*, said Stendhal's female characters are "too romantic." (Stendhal had written earlier in *Of Love* that Goethe is an example of middle-class stuffiness, and I am sure, from Goethe's knowledge of the equally obscure then *The Red and the Black* of a few years later, that Goethe, who also never wrote publicly, only in letters, about

Stendhal, had read that treatise.) What was Stendhal to do with idiots as his contemporaries, and posterities: we may be the only writer in the this language, in post-Stendhal English-language criticism, who puts Stendhal on par with Shakespeare and *far* above Tolstoy and Dostoevsky....
)

as the novel is in *depth of characterization, analytic thought, and philosophy*; its portrayal of religion as *mere politics*, and nothing more; its exceptionally acute and vivid characterizations of even the secondary figures, such as the virtuous Abbé Chélan and Father Pirard, the corrupt cleric Frilair, Marquis de la Mole, the handsome, perfectly refined, and polite, but politically fanatical Bishop of Agde, Fouqué, M. de Rênal who turns in the course of the novel from being the Royalist mayor of his town to a Liberal opposition man, matters in France having turned a deadly turn, Valenod, that gigantic character who wants to sleep with Mme de Rênal, and who is cleverly and clearly out-maneuvered by her and Julien's use of his personal note paper to deceive her husband: what a marvelous novel!, *et al*, matters that were comprehensible to a true scholar such as Auerbach. Truly, *The Red and the Black* equals *Othello*, in style, wit, originality; and emotional depth as well.

4. *War and Peace*

(translation by Ann Dunnigan)

from Book, Part Five, chapter 1,

"He read and read, anything that came to hand, so that coming home he picked up a book even while his valets were still taking off his clothes; from sleep he proceeded to the idle talk of drawing rooms and his Club, then to carousing and women, and back to gossip, reading, and wine. Drinking became more and more a physical and at the same time a moral necessity for him. Although the doctors had warned him that with his corpulence wine was dangerous, he drank heavily. He had a sense of well-being only when, after tossing several glasses of wine down his capacious gullet, he experienced a pleasant warmth in his body, an affability toward all his fellows, and a readiness to respond to every superficial idea without going into it very deeply. Only after emptying a bottle or two did he dimly feel that the terrible, tangled skein of life, which had appalled him before, was not so dreadful as he had fancied. He was always conscious of some aspect of that skein, as, with a buzzing in his head after dinner or supper, he chatted or listened to conversation or read. But it was only under the influence of wine that he could say to himself: "It doesn't matter. I will unravel it—I have a solution all ready. But I have no time now—I'll think it out later." But that *later* never came.

"In the morning, on an empty stomach, all the old questions remained as insoluble as ever, and Pierre hastily snatched up a book, and was delighted if someone came to see him.

"Sometimes he remembered that soldiers in a shelter under enemy fire, when they have nothing to do, make some effort to find some occupation the more easily endure the danger. And it seemed to Pierre that all men were like these soldiers, seeking a refuge from life: some in ambition, some in cards, some in women, in wine, in playthings, horses, sports, and some in politics or government affairs. 'Nothing is trivial, nothing important—it's all the same: one should only try to escape from it as well as one can,' thought Pierre. 'If only one didn't see *it*, that terrible *it*.'"

While *Madame Bovary*, in our happy youth, made us feel that we should become a writer, not because we admired that heap of garbage, but because it seemed so easy to surpass it, it was *War and Peace*, and that novel alone, then, that made us *feel* that literary composition could have meaning.

Tolstoy's strength lie in his characterization of his main male characters, Pierre, Lyovin (in *Anna Karenina*), Andrei, Nikolai, and in his depictions of battles, which Tolstoy said he learned to visualize in literary form from Stendhal's chapters set in Waterloo in *The Charterhouse of Parma*; in fact, in his biography of Tolstoy, Ernest Simmons describes an evening at the Tolstoy household, when Tolstoy was rather aged; he was holding forth to the crowd in his drawing room on the virtues of Dickens; one of the attendees asked Tolstoy, "I suppose Dickens had the greatest influence on you?" Tolstoy replied, "No, the writer who influenced me most is Stendhal." I think it is in the same biography that an event is recounted, again from Tolstoy's later years; Tolstoy told a devotee that he had just finished rereading *The Red and the Black*, and *finally* had come to discover what was the main problem with Stendhal, but, as I recall, either Tolstoy did not, or the biographer does not, elaborate. I would *die to know* what *Tolstoy* thought it was, because this would have been *most* **illuminating**.

Tolstoy's *fatal* weakness is his female characters, Natasha, Sonia (in a chapter in *War and Peace*, Nikolai tells Sonia he will marry her, runs in the snow to Natasha and tells his sister of this; later in the day, Natasha plays a "game" of looking into a glass, a "game" that she takes *solemnly*, and *sees*, then asks Sonia to do the same; Sonia sees nothing, and is even unsure whether she is supposed to see Nikolai there, or Natasha's beloved, Prince Andrei. Sonia says she saw "him" in the posture of lying down. Natasha asks, "Was Andrei wounded?" oh my god type of thing. No, replies Sonia, lying. That night, Tolstoy writes, after these excitations, Natasha slept in a such-such manner: Joyce told Arthur Power, the latter recalls in his memoir about his friendship with Joyce, that Dostoevsky has broken apart the "simpering maidens" of Victorian fiction—I would say that though Dostoevsky owes a little to Dante and Goethe (Gretchen tells Faust, "You must believe," and this duty to convert the reprobate male is done more subtly in *Crime and Punishment*, with actual psychology and deeper artistry:

Nabokov was revolted, as his lectures show, by the scene of Raskolnikov and Sonya bending over the New Testament, as she is trying to convert him: what rot, thought Nabokov: the christ had forgiven the prostitute two thousand years ago, but not the murderer, a nice point; all I would say is that Raskolnikov is *not* converted, and the raggedness of the scene is finely psychological), he made it all his very own: all I find in Tolstoy are such simpering maidens of Victorian-era literature), Marya, Dolly, Kitty—even Austen's Elizabeth Bennet and Anne Elliott, who obey their parents and consider *very* seriously the financial wherewithal of their potential "betrotheds," are more charismatic than Tolstoy's young women in the two famous novels); the one exception, the overrated Anna Karenina, is neither as attractively bold and independent an adulteress as Mme de Rênal, nor as fiercely abundant and alive and ferociously life-loving a character as Molly, in Joyce, who may not cut as deeply into life in *Ulysses* as Tolstoy does in *War and Peace*, and *that* novel *alone*—certainly not in *Anna Karenina*, a novel that, as philosophy and as art, is far inferior to *Ulysses* and *Pale Fire*—but whom I prefer as a writer to Tolstoy.

5. *Crime and Punishment*

We believe that Chekhov, Bunin, Nabokov, and other similar *Russians* were consumed with envy when they claimed to look down a little or lot on Dostoevsky's styles and techniques. This novel proceeds more rapidly than any other (except *The Charterhouse of Parma*) we have ever read, much more than the "super-thrillers" being sold as

top bestsellers: compared to it, *The Bourne Identity* (1980) of Robert Ludlum, the best of such high sellers of the past fifty years, made even more famous in the last decade or two by a film franchise based on its male lead character, does not come close to the pace of Dostoevsky in *Crime and Punishment*. Most astonishing is that Dostoevsky manages this headlong reading experience while having his characters merely think, walk, and talk.
(translation by Sidney Monas)

from Part Two, chapter 6

"Listen, dear gentleman!" the girl called out behind him.

"What?"

She was embarrassed.

"Dear gentleman, I'd always be glad to spend some hours with you, but just now, somehow, you make me feel shy. Wouldn't you give me six kopeks, my handsome cavalier, for a little drink?"

Raskolnikov gave her whatever he could fish out of his pocket. Three five-kopek coins.

"Ah, what a kind, good gentleman!"

"What's your name?"

"Just ask for Duclida."

"Well, how do you like that!" one of the group suddenly remarked, shaking her head at Duclida "I don't know what it takes to beg like that! Why, I'd drop through the sidewalk for shame. …"

Raskolnikov gazed curiously at the speaker. She was pock-marked, about thirty, with black and blue marks on her face and a swollen upper lip. She was quiet and earnest as she spoke.

"Where is it," thought Raskolnikov, as he walked on, "where is it I was reading somebody condemned to death said or thought an hour before his death that if he had to live somewhere on a crag, on a cliff, on a narrow ledge where his two feet could hardly stand, and all around there'd be the abyss, the ocean, everlasting darkness, everlasting solitude, and an everlasting storm, and he had to remain like that—standing on a square yard of space—all his life, a thousand years, an eternity, it would still be better to live like that than die at the moment. To live and to live and to live and to live! No matter how you live, if only to live. How true that is! God, how true! What a scoundrel man is! And he's a scoundrel who calls him a scoundrel for that!" he added a minute later.

He came out on another street. "Bah! The Crystal Palace! Razumikhin was talking about the Crystal Palace. What the hell was I after, though? Oh, yes...."

6. *The Karamazov Brothers*

Not as narratively super-charged as *Crime and Punishment*, and boring in parts (Father Zosima in it is a *total* bore— like the **monotone** *theoretical historian* to whom Tolstoy unfortunately gave fully one third of the otherwise marvelous *War and Peace*; goes on and on, the narrative about that flunkey: Stendhal, in both *Rouge* and *Chartreuse* can deliver a pious cleric or two to the reader, with ten times the force of Dostoevsky, *in a stroke or two*: he can *also* show the worldly yet still honest prelate, *something rather* *beyond Dostoevsky's conceptions in **this** novel*: the Bishop who gives a set of Tacitus to Julien for his successes in the seminary examinations, with the conspiracy against Julien in mind), necessary for the novel's ambitions, as Dostoevsky ambitiously thought of them. Philosophically it is even more profoundly questioning than *Crime and Punishment*, with questions that are nearly, if not completely, impossible to answer, if put in general terms, outside of Russian Orthodox Christianity,

After Smerdyakov has made the "sinful" statement that were he forced by "heathen" Muhammadan Turks to deny his "Baptism" and "Christ" and, as critical for Dostoevsky as Christianity, Russia, he would do so as it is only rational, an idea repeated in dialogue form *ad nauseam* (repetition in Dostoevsky, as in Tolstoy, a necessary mechanism, that would be true weakness (it slightly is, still) were it not done for the purpose of *power*)) to which his father, whom he will murder in the course of the novel, responds with scorn. Smerdyakov says, addressing all, but in specific a hireling,

(Avsey's translation of what he renders accurately as *The Karamazov Brothers*, rather than *The Brothers Karamazov*)

   "It may very well be the situation, just work it out for yourself, Grigory Vasilyevich, that's where the rub is. After all, if I really had believed as one should believe at that time, then, true enough, it would have been sinful to go over to the heathen religion of Muhammad rather than accept martyrdom for my faith. But the point is that there wouldn't have been any martyrdom in that case because, sir, all I'd have needed to do at that moment would have been to say to the mountain: 'Move and crush my persecutors,' and at that instant it would have moved and crushed them like cockroaches, and I'd have gone off as if nothing had happened, chanting and glorifying God. But then again, what if at that very moment I had put all this to the test and deliberately cried out to the mountain, 'Crush these torturers!' and it hadn't crushed them. Well then, tell me, how could I have stopped myself being assailed by doubts, especially with me being in a state of mortal terror? And so, knowing full well that I wouldn't enter the Kingdom of Heaven (for the mountain hadn't moved at my command) ...'" [end of chapter 7, titled "Controversy," of Part One].

As I suggested, this has connotation beyond the matter being discussed. If Mr. Rushdie, who has publicly stated that he is an atheist, were in the hands of Ayatollah Khamenei, current ruler of Iran, and Khamenei said, cleanse yourself with water on your arms and in your nostrils, etc., by doing the rituals prescribed in Islam in the manner in which prayers are to be readied for, or for the touching of the Muhammadan scripture book, etc., and renounce atheism, apologize to the world, renounce being a novelist, short story writer, and essayist, and read this book The Holy Quran with commentary chosen by me aloud in front of cameras transmitting internationally your devoutness, what should Mr. Rushdie, who has been in hiding for decades, fearing justifiably for his life, and who was attacked brutally a year ago, do? Dostoevsky, the anti-Semite, the supporter of church and tsar, the doctrinarian Christian, the supporter of Russoslavs ruling over all Slavs, posing a question that Plato, Aristotle, Hume, Hobbes, Voltaire, famous philosophers, never dared to ask.

More Shakespeares ((*Twelfth Night*, *Macbeth*) and Stendhal's *The Charterhouse of Parma* (perfect narrative art, sweeping and *rapid*. Clear and subtly moving. The final two paragraphs were *imitated without acknowledgment* by Flaubert (who, in his letters, can be seen to have read Stendhal's novel when he *began* writing *Madame Bovary*, and professed to despise Stendhal, *that despicable man, Flaubert*) in the simply idiotic and merely *pretty* and superficial *Madame Bovary*, in *its* last two or three paragraphs. Our favorite name, among all literary characters', appears in this novel, *Riscara*. We wish it was our father's family name. Sounds like the name of a majestic Italian poet.)) should be put in, but places must be left for other *very* fine writers.

7. *Ulysses*

The three successive scenes-chapters in it, the Dubliners tracked-in-parallel scene, the Ormond scene with its perfect balance of musical juggling and repetitions of words, just jagged enough under the frieze of flowing prose to convey exactly a very precise *invented* sense of morbid nervousness in Bloom who knows that his wife is being had by Boylan at that very time in his marriage bed, and which scene ends with respective expulsions from within the body, posterior for Bloom to Boylan's anterior one left to the imagination, of organic substance, and the hour of imagined real betrayal and that actual betrayal by his wife are in the last word of the scene-chapter "Done," and the loonily gobbledygook political sanity of the citizen scene that is rightly the historical climax of *Ulysses*, after which a Shakespeare would have stopped with a book even more lucid than *Pale Fire*.

8. *Ficciones*

Though Borges may not have possessed the wit of Nabokov at the latter's best (in *Pale Fire*, and only in that novel, ten times funnier than Proust or *Lolita*), with passages as boisterously funny in it as,

"As to my own activities, they were I am afraid most unsatisfactory from all points of view—emotional, creative, and social. That jinxy streak had started on the eve when I had been kind enough to offer a young friend—a candidate for my third ping-pong table who after a sensational series of traffic violations had been deprived of his driving licence—to take him, in my powerful Kramler, all the way to his parents' estate, a little matter of two hundred miles. In the course of an all-night party, among crowds of strangers—young people, old people, cloyingly perfumed girls—in an atmosphere of fireworks, barbecue smoke, horseplay, jazz music, and auroral swimming, I loss all contact with the silly boy, was made to dance, was made to sing, got involved in the most boring bibble-babble imaginable with various relatives of the child, and finally, in some inconceivable manner, found myself transported to a different party on a different estate, where, after some indescribable parlor games, in which my beard was nearly snipped off, I had a fruit-and-rice breakfast, and was taken by an anonymous host…."

or the clean, neat prose of Hemingway (from "Up in Michigan")

JIM GILMORE CAME TO HORTON BAY from Canada. He bought the blacksmith shop from old man Horton. Jim was short and dark with black mustaches and big hands. He was a good horseshoer and did not look much like a blacksmith even with his leather apron on. He lived upstairs above the blacksmith shop and took his meals at D.J. Smith's.

Liz Coates worked for Smith's. Mrs. Smith, who was a very large clean woman, said Liz Coates was the neatest girl she'd ever seen. Liz had good legs and always wore clean gingham aprons and Jim noticed that her hair was always neat behind her. He liked her face because it was so jolly but he never thought about her.

Liz liked Jim very much. She liked it the way he walked over from the shop and often went to the kitchen door to watch for him to start down the road. She liked it about his mustache. She liked it about how white his teeth were when he smiled. She liked it very much that he didn't look like a blacksmith. She liked it how much D.J. Smith and Mrs. Smith liked Jim. One day she found that she liked it the way the hair was black on his arms and how white they were above the tanned line when he washed up in the washbasin outside the house. Liking that made her feel funny.

, but *Ficciones* has even more piquant, intense, trenchant, moving passages than anything by Proust, Woolf, Camus, Nabokov, Hemingway, or Beckett (who merely combined, as has been noted *by many*, Cartesian Christianity with Schopenhauerian Buddhism—but, like Proust, Woolf, and Camus, he has an interesting, if, finally, minor style),

Translation by Borges and di Giovanni.

from "The Approach to al-Mu'tasim" in *Ficciones*,

"Its central figure—whose name we are never told—is a law student in Bombay. Blasphemously, he disbelieves in the Islamic faith of his fathers, but on the tenth night of the moon of Muharram, he finds himself in the midst of a civil disorder between Muslims and Hindus. It is a night of drums and prayers. Among the mob of the heathen, the great paper canopies of the Muslim procession force their way. A hail of Hindu bricks flies down from a roof terrace. A knife is sunk into a belly. Someone—Muslim? Hindu?—dies and is trampled on. Three thousand men are fighting—stick against revolver, obscenity against curse, God the Indivisible against the many Gods. Instinctively, the student freethinker joins in the fighting. With his bare hands, he kills (or thinks he has killed) a Hindu. The Government police—mounted, thunderous, and barely awake—intervene, dealing impartial whiplashes. The student flees, almost under the legs of the horses, heading for the farthest ends of town. He crosses two sets of railroad tracks, or the same tracks twice."

This "fabulist," as he is often termed, Borges, is, face it, in this collection of tales, as "realistic" and large a mental stratosphere as Joyce in *Ulysses*, with or without the latter's quite dead second half ("Dead, quite dead," as Josef Tura tells his wife regarding the fate of the spy, Siletsky, in Lubitsch's *To Be or Not To Be*)—except for the last page or page and a half of the second Sandymount beach scene, a scene that begins with the "word," "Ba," and concludes with its

Cuckoo
Cuckoo
Cuckoo

chiming nine o'clock at night, and reminding the reader that Bloom's had his pathetic little *revenge* for being cuckolded earlier that day; and except for Molly's forty-page monologue ending *Ulysses*.

9. *The Iliad*

We do not put Homer higher, because, in spite of the magnificent poetry of the first six and the last six "books" of *The Iliad*, not matched by that in any part of the slimmer-weighted *The Odyssey*, his figures, unlike those of Kurosawa (the unit in Kurosawa is *the film*; once one is finished, and it has to been seen in entirety, the only pictures so, another Kurosawa cannot be viewed *for many hours*; the unit in Motoki Noriko is *the episode*, even if the viewing period of one is only a couple of minutes with her in it, since the rest of *Denjin Zaboga* is safely ignorable; one is exhausted by the intellectual effort necessary for a single episode alone), Stendhal, Shakespeare, Titian,

Titian, *The Flaying of Marsyas* (circa., 1570-1576)

Titian, *Tarquin and Lucretia* (1570)

(compare with

Michelangelo, Sistine Chapel, *Jeremiah*

Michelangelo, Sistine Chapel, *Ezekiel*

, *as dramatic as* Titian, but compositionally much *simpler* in attempting to get the visual impact across, both pairs.

In psychological depth of portraiture, there is simply no comparison between Michelangelo and Titian. Let the reader decide (Michelangelo's panel, *Creation of Heaven and Earth*, facial details of a collage of Michelangelo's sculptures (including an elderly self-portrait) vs. Titian's *Portrait of Jacopo Strada*, and *Portrait of Pope Paul III with His Grandsons*, a deadly piece, as the pope and one of at least one of the grandsons did not realize),

"VS."

)

, Tolstoy (the five supreme *male* artists and *thinkers*),
[Michelangelo, Dostoevsky—all religions currently
extant, for which we can speak, are *ascetic*, including *holi-*

paint-dousing on each other and dancing hinduism, and islam [Stendhal on islam, in his book *Of Love*, "Muhammad was a *puritan*. He proscribed pleasures that are of no harm to anyone. He has killed love in those lands that have embraced islam."], and they go against the full human spirit, trying to limit that divine gift of *nature*, and so they produce unhappiness and *suffering*, if fully believed in **and** *fully* followed (so many, so *many*, religious people *seem*, at least, to be mildly comfortable and *happy*, but *this is only because they* **unconscionably** *do not follow* **all** *the principles and actions* **required** *(I repeat,* **required***) by their religious creed or their "***God***"*): christiantiy is unique in having produced honest men (the example of a **true** christian woman, *true to her faith*, is, I suppose, even with all her ironies, the greatest American poet, Emily Dickinson, who lived largely by herself, and *suffered* in her soul) who did *both*, believe *and* follow, for different reasons each (Lyof Tolstoy also suffered, but largely out of his sexual impulses—put into his characters Pierre and Lyovin, the latter of whom confesses (as Tolstoy, in his own life, had earlier) to his bride, Kitty, immediately after their marriage, his immoral desires for and acts regarding women, before he married her, but this consideration exists *outside* of religion, for having powerful lust can bother *a pure atheist* as well): Dostoevsky, for a wider philosophical reason, and Michelangelo, for his persistence in believing in the *harmful* fairy tales of bible as "noble," **truly suffered**, as witness Michelangelo's self-portrait in sculpture, above: the two greatest religious-cum-philosophic men: Dostoevsky is more scalpel-like, Michelangelo has more grandeur and depth to his suffering, for he, though proud of his art, did not have the equivalent of Dostoevsky's *literary vanity*, which was *very* easily wounded, leading to words and actions, and such things as the false modesty in praising his own book when he wrote that Hugo's *Les Misérable*, though "widely esteemed less than my *Crime and Punishment*, is the better book." What about Moslem writers, such as Rumi, Hafiz, al-Mutannabbi, ibn 'Arabi, Firdausi, Rumi, Hafiz, Saadi, Omar Khayyam, Ghalib, Iqbal, the reader may ask. Certainly, most of them, according to the biographies that have survived, enjoyed life, as islam is supposedly a less ascetic religion, than the "O ye, abandon this world of *illusions/falsehoods*" brand found in buddhism, in hinduism, in christianity. But before we proceed further, let us see what quran itself says on the topic of poetry. Here is the crucial passage, perhaps the only one in quran, on poetry: Surah 26, verses 223-227: "And as for the poets - [they, too, are prone to deceive themselves: and so, only] those who are lost in grievous error would follow them. Art thou not aware that they roam confusedly through all the valleys [of words and thoughts], and that they [so often] say what they do not do [or feel]? [Most of them are of this kind -] save those who have attained to faith, and do righteous deeds, and remember God unceasingly, and defend themselves [only] after having been wronged and [trust in God's promise that] those who are bent on wrong doing will in time come to know how evil a turn their destinies are bound to take!" Taking this as TRUTH, one wishes to ask al-Mutannabbi, famed Arab composer of the following lines of poetry,

"

My heart is aflame, burning with love for you
While your heart is frigid-cold toward me
You think so lightly of me, treating me with indifference
My soul is sickened, my body debilitated
"

Etc.

Now, Allah cannot be "frigid-cold" toward a poet who loves Him.

Q.E.D. al-Mutannabbi, that revered "moslem" Arab poet, is singing of an *earthly* beloved.

   A thousand years later moslem poets are still writing *exactly the same thing*, **in exactly the same manner,** of all religions' followers, *moslems* have sung *most* of **alcohol** (because prohibited by their Allah), the other theme of their insultingly same similes, pronounced by the poet as an original contribution to earlier moslem writing! O infidel al-Mutannabbi, ibn 'Arabi, Firdausi, Rumi, Hafiz, Saadi, Omar Khayyam, Ghalib, Iqbal, O ye moslems, poetry, which you practics'd with abandon and *delight, was* **forbidden** *you by Allah*, unless it dealt solely, and **solely**, with Allah, **without** *evil-beings'-inspired metaphors, similes, and invented conceits. Did you not even read the quran* **once, O ye hell-bounds?** Poetry (and, so, also, lyrics, to be set to music) is *forbidden* in quran, unless the poet, as quran says, "remember God **unceasingly**," **unceasingly**, the quran could not be clearer, which means songs (called *naat*) and poetry that remember Muhammad are *forbidden*, also; painting, drawing, and music are *forbidden* in hadiths. Allah and His Prophet have spoken on the subject of art, with no vagueness in their wordings: if Muslim are to obey them, they must give up art, and not be happy writing poems on love, beauty, wine, nature, or the Prophet, nor should they make music, nor sing, nor draw the likeness of a horse or a man: it is Allah's religion, after all, not any Muslim's prerogative to question Him. As for myself, I write philosophy, which nowhere in quran is forbidden. A Hindu, if he was one, has given us *Ramayana*, that beautiful poem, which, in its Critical Edition, derived by modern hindu scholars (taking in all the *corrupt* texts of it that exist, hundreds of versions) gave to the world, before reprobate and low-brow Indians, since ancient times, recognizing the palpable greatness of the work, began to add to and subtract from, its immortal form. Jews include such great artists as Heine, who converted to christianity, so that in Israel, concerning a place or occasion commemorating Jews who made major contributions to history, there was a great controversy whether to include Heine among great Jews of the past, ending with proscribing him, I think! Certainly, the most famous and influential Jew in history, along with Albert Einstein and Adolf Hitler (**he** was granted by "Fate" the *singular* honor of having *forever* **annihilated** the one great civilization that had ever), **was not even considered**, I am *sure* (no sirree, no boy, not in good old, not in *my*, Israel: we hate that "Jew," that "traitor"; perhaps, I am wrong: the reader can research that occasion when Heine became controversial, and *see for him- herself* what blasted Jews did: in fact, the man predicted *the future* (and so was in *this regard*, truly a *prophet*): "a prophet is not without honour except…."), Jesus: **this** is the totally and *incurably* *sick* and small-racist, you-must-own-up-to-your inheritance and *obey*, Jewish ethnicity: truly sickening, if you think of it— I am not fluent in German, and read Heine only in translation: about Heine, Nietzsche, who is considered by **many German scholars** as *the greatest prose stylist of the language*, wrote (in his autobiography, *Ecce Homo*, Part Two, chapter 4), "The highest concept of the lyrical poet was given to me by *Heinrich Heine*. I seek in vain in all the realms of history for an equally sweet and passionate music. He possessed that divine malice without which I cannot imagine perfection. I estimate the value of men, of races, according to the necessity by which they cannot imagine the god apart from the satyr.

"And how he handles his German! One day it will be said that Heine and I have been by far the foremost artists of the German language—at an incalculable distance from everything mere Germans have done with it." Since it is the greatest German prose stylist writing this, I am *confirmed* in my own experience of reading German poetry *in translation*, that Heine is *incomparably* superior to Goethe, Schiller, Mörike, Klopstock, and Rilke; even to Hölderlin, the other great German poet, after Heine, who is not *too* loved in earlier, or perhaps even, contemporary (considering its hero-worship of Goethe) Germany, because he was born a *Jew*, not adored by Germans and rejected by Israelis, the greatest German poet, *born* a Jew!—, Proust, an atheist who had *great* interest in church steeples and stained windows in old French churches, but none in synagogues, and who pictures Sodom and Gomorrah as ideal abodes where intense pangs of jealousy and joy are to be found, and Ophuls, who begins and ends his greatest picture, *Madame de*, with the image of different forms of a cross; and a Jewish scientist, Einstein, who wrote in a letter some facts, one of which has changed, *proving* his point, "As far as my experience goes, they are in fact no better than other human groups, even if they are protected from the worst excesses by a lack of power. Otherwise, I cannot perceive anything 'chosen' about them." Of course, *now* they have power in Israel ("protected from the worst excesses by a lack of power"), a protectorate, as Guam is, of America, and commit atrocious, murderous crimes (called "non-felonies" by American governments, of Republicans and Democrats alike—the two are most alike, despite what one hears in journalistic trash: one says 5% tax rate, the other, 4.75%; one says 3 trillion dollars of aid to Israel, the other says, 2.99 trillion dollars of such aid: and it is still called a "multi-party democracy," what a farce!: I lived there for fifteen years, and not only *couldn't* vote and *didn't want* to—*Youjinbou* and *The Hidden Fortress*, eternal visions) against moslems: Einstein was right on the spot. Einstein also wrote, "The word God is for me nothing more than the expression and product of human weaknesses, the Bible a collection of honourable, but still primitive, legends which are nevertheless pretty childish." (Einstein, taught since childhood in schools around the world: one day they may start teaching *all* his thoughts to little schoolboys and little schoolgirls, so they can go home and ask their parents, "Mommy, Dad, why did you lie to us? Who are you compared to Einstein in *intellect*? What, in your God's name, have you done with *your* life?" .... I don't have much hope for mankind: democracy *inevitably* creates *severe* forms of *censorship*: one of the *least free* political systems) Buddhism has produced Kurosawa, that man with a *violently infectious* sense of humor about life. Buddha himself thought: "Life is suffering only." I.e., great ethnic Jews and a great buddhist simply ignored judaism and buddhism, respectively, and triumphed thereby. No drum-thumping and featherdancing witchdoctor of Native America has produced anything of artistic or *intellectual* worth, though *the people themselves* are very *peaceable* and *good*, unlike Jews, and victims of a christian ("Manifest Destiny") genocide, worthy of Stalin and Hitler.], Joyce, Borges, Proust, and even Milton's Satan, Adam, and Eve, are one or *at most* two trait-motive characters, and do not have individualized, *subtle* consciousnesses. Homer came too early in history to have had a developed sense of the inner human.

10. Pale Fire

This novel divides readers and scholars alike along the lines of interpretation, viz., Shadeans and Kinbotians. The latter read the novel as it seems to be, the poem by Shade, and an introduction, commentary, and index by Kinbote (really, according to most readers, and Nabokov, the "interviewee," a professor named Botkin, with Shakespearean ghosts). The former claim that the entire work is a composition of Shade, the poet; he invents Kinbote, the commentary, and the rest.

We are no scholar, but merely a novelist, but it seems to us, indubitably, to our small novelist's mind, that either reading makes no difference. If the former, then the novel is as it is. Or, the latter case, the novel is as it is, except that Shade and Nabokov are exactly parallel, with only this distinction that Nabokov also invents Shade inventing *Pale Fire*. They both invent the whole affair (including, obviously, the family and family life of Shade, who must, to get the work published, acknowledge directly to the publisher and public, that he is alive and there is no Kinbote, a man with the delusion that he is the deposed king of Zembla, and so the novel is really the novel of Shade, which breaks apart the theory. However, it is possible that Shadeans are more well founded: this would make Nabokov *a weaker writer* than we think he is, because the plot is then implausible, but makes John Shade one of the most intelligent characters in literature, on par with Hamlet and Conte Mosca, though not with Iago and Julien.

We must say that we suspect that Nabokov had no idea when he published the novel that the Shadean theory would ever appear in literary criticism. It did not in Mary McCarthy early review, which established the prestige of the novel, but Nabokov made a relevant point about her review, some of the plums in the pudding in it were hers alone. Many interpretations never imagined by Nabokov appear.

We understand now, and finally, why Nabokov was very reticent when it came to himself speaking of *Pale Fire*, why he was not so when speaking himself of *Lolita* and *Ada*, why he translated the former into Russian himself and personally supervised very closely and carefully that of the latter into French. He, as a self-consciously careful defender of his reputation, sensed the comparative weakness of these other two, in relation to *Pale Fire*, a novel of ideas and intellect (a class of writing he claimed never to have composed), unlike those phenomena of style. It could survive a literal translation by another hand.

Pale Fire should be called "*Proof Through* **Demonstration** *of Afterlife*," since more than a being a novel (for Nabokov posits *artistic inspiration* as the *sole* proof of afterlife, ultimately), it is in the category of the "proofs of god's existence" by Aquinas and Descartes, though *far more* successful as a work of ***philosophy***. Like Stendhal's *Rouge* and Plato's dialogues, it is philosophy, disguised as *devilishly* powerful narrative. "Pale Fires" are the pale lights bobbing around, ghosts, that Shade's daughter sees in the barn, which warn her, in code—art always being in need of *correct* analysis (from *Pale Fire*, "To this statement, my dear poet would probably not have subscribed, but, for better of for worse, it is the commentator who has the last word." Last line of Kinbote's "Foreword"—, of her father's future assassination, and how to prevent it—the quite devastating Nabokovian *genius*: to have Kinbote ("bare bodkin"), who possesses Hazel's notes from the nights at the barn, writes that they are so *unimportant* that he shall not transcribe the rest!—and only *peripherally* are the lines from Shakespeare's *Timon of Athens*, which *also are found* in *Hamlet* ("And 'gins to pale his ineffectual fire"), where ***a Ghost also appears***. Nabokov's wife, noting that this had been missed altogether by *all* critics, who ignorantly were instead "analyzing" the junk about Shade being the *actual* composer of the novel by a "gamesman" novelist etc., wrote in her introduction, lightly, to her translation of *Pale Fire* into *Russian*, that her husband's interest in the *hereafter* had been overlooked. She was, of course, *always* privy to Nabokov's full intents in his novels.

Even the greatest nineteenth century writers, who were, *pace* Pushkin and Goethe, all novelists, did not comprehend the *crucial importance of **re-readability***. Very few non-scholars, who reread those only because they write articles or books on them and are *paid* for doing so, would want to reread *War and Peace*, *The Red and the Black*, *Crime and Punishment, from beginning to end*, without stopping for another book. The first reading experience is the best in their case. From Shakespeare, from Dante, Joyce learned that re-readability is critical in making a work of literature (or, for that matter, cinema) supreme. Nabokov went so far as to say, in his lectures to his Cornell students, published posthumously, "Curiously enough, you cannot read a book. You can only reread it." And *Pale Fire,* like *Ulysses* and *Ficciones*, is much more re-readable than the best of Stendhal, Tolstoy, and Dostoevsky. Even *Don Quixote* is not as pleasurable to re-go through, and, so, easier to reread than the "realists," so-called, including the "experimental" Faulkner.

I first read *The Red and the Black* at seventeen, and howled with tears and joys, by its end; starting with Julien's trip back to the countryside, with the intent of assassinating Mme de Rênal; I read it again, in entirety, at nineteen, and it was a piece of cold, logical analysis—it did not move me emotionally any longer. The same with *Anna Karenina*, etc.

I still dip into Borges, Nabokov, and Joyce—*and* Proust, "Too long, much too long," as Josef Tura, pretending to be that spy, Siletski, tells the Gestapo colonel, Colonel Erhardt (finally, the actor, Sig Ruman, *vulgarized* in the overrated Marx Brothers' pictures, and *sentimentalized* in others, even by Hawks, in his sentimental melodrama, *Only Angels Have Wings*, was given a role with *juice*, and did he rise to the occasion!), when asked by him, "Tell me, how long has it been since you last saw the Fuhrer?"—, one volume each of these writers' (one-book writers, all three) works, and get the same adventure— sans the *difficulty of reading them the first time around*—as ever, without ever having been *moved* by them.

Joyce's greatest superiority to Borges and Nabokov is his *far* greater depth of characterization, of Bloom, of Molly, of Buck Mulligan, and a few others; they are *far* less deadlily obscure (I once, in 1995, advised a student who, in the first stages of a course that I gave to a class of university students, a male student, who had given the most intelligent answers to the questions in the first of three examinations in the course, "Do read *Ulysses*, if you are interested in the kinds of books I teach." He smiled awkwardly, as if to say, "You know that no one can understand that awfully difficult book."—I taught *Joseph Andrews*, *Pride and Prejudice*, *Wuthering Heights*, *Bleak House*, *The Sound and the Fury*, and *Lolita*, knowing that *Pale Fire* and *Ulysses* would take too much time to explain in an "Introduction to Fiction" class) than Joyce can sometimes, to the exasperation of the most faithful of his readers, be.

This is to say Shakespeare is as *profound*, at least, as Dostoevsky, Tolstoy, and Stendhal, and as *re-readable*, at least, as Nabokov, Borges, and Joyce.

II

1

Freud: Psychiatry

No better examples of the incestuous relationship between the media and the people it purports to explain objectively, than of two twentieth century frauds, Freud and Picasso. Freud and his theory that the mind *represses into the directly-unknown unconscious* (but knowable through the interpretation of dreams) the sexual desire of a male child for his mother, the Oedipus complex, as this Austrian doctor called it, a well-known description by him of it in one of his most celebrated books, "[Oedipus'] destiny moves us only because it might have been ours— because the oracle laid the same curse upon us before our birth as upon him. It is the fate of all of us, perhaps, to direct our first sexual impulse towards our mother and our first hatred and our first murderous wish against our father. Our dreams convince us that this is so. King Oedipus who slew his father Laïus and married his mother Jocasta, merely shows us the fulfillment of our childhood wishes.... Here is one in whom these primaeval wishes of our childhood have been fulfilled, and we shrink back from him with the whole force of the *repression* [italics ours, by the way] by which those wishes have since that time been held down within us." Freud did not actually possess an intricately *perceiving* mind, a sorry state for one ambitious in the cause of psychology. As for repression, the central concept in Freud: Stendhal wrote in one of his two autobiographies,

"My mother, Mme Henriette Gagnon, was a charming woman and I was in love with my mother.

"I must hurriedly add that I lost her when I was seven.

"When I loved her at about the age of six, in 1789, I showed exactly the same characteristics as in 1828 when I was madly in love with Alberthe de Rubempré. My way of pursuing happiness was basically unchanged; there was just this difference: I was, as regards the physical side of love, just as Caesar would be, if he came back into the world, as regards the use of cannon and small arms. I would have learned very quickly, and my tactics would have remained basically the same.

"I wanted to cover my mother with kisses, and without any clothes on. She loved me passionately and often kissed me."

Q.E.D. There is no such phenomenon as "repression into the unconscious."

Similar stuff may be written of Picasso who has been dubbed by twentieth century hacks—starting with the self-proclaimed "genius" Gertrude Stein (the *Alice B Toklas* autobiography junk was not even original in its title, for unknown to this *uneducated* **woman** was this historical incident that the Afghan-area poet Rumi, before Dante was born, had penned a book of Persian *ghazals*, which on the title page ascribed its authorship to his male lover of that time: Miss Stein who thought that the utter sham, Picasso, was a genius *only* surpassed in powers of the *spirit* by Miss Stein *herself*? As one person I have had the pleasure to know said, "Stein asked, 'Why do people read Joyce? I was playing with words long before him,' when Shakespeare (not to mention Lewis Carroll) was playing with words, in English, long before her"—, and by their sheer imitators in this one, a "genius." According to these same people, Stendhal is a "Romanto-realistic" novelist merely describing "men and manners in 1830" (the title of *one* of *The Red and the Black*'s chapters), *not* one or two of the supreme psychologists in world history, at large, but Freud is a "scientific" psychologist!

Idealists, Recent and Ancient

As for the "most celebrated" psychologist-philosopher of the second half of the previous century, Michel Foucault, this is a typical passage by him

(the passage from Foucault's *Discipline, Punish*, about to be quoted, after this parenthesis ends, reads more like Kafka's *In the Penal Settlement—without the genius:* let me explain *in a digression* what I mean by "without the genius."

Digression aforementioned:

Begins the Comedy of Dante Alighieri, Florentine in birth, not in custom (the poem by Dante Alighieri, who, *in his ideas*, is *merely* rhymed *Summa Theologiae*, as Singleton, his critic in America, has so *unwittingly* demonstrated in his commentary to the translation, by himself: no originality in anything except *representation of imagery*: that those in hell, as described and evoked in *Inferno*, can see the future but do not know the present—so that whenever the Day of Judgment arrives they will have *no* knowledge of present or future whatever: *this* is genius: but consider his *pallid* picture of the Christian "god" in *Paradiso*, *even* as *imagery*: Dante the wayfarer has just seen that god: (translation by Charles Singleton) "A single moment makes for me greater oblivion than five and twenty centuries have wrought upon the enterprise that made Neptune wonder at the shadow of the Argo. Thus my mind, all rapt, was gazing, fixed, motionless and intent, ever enkindled by it gazing. In that Light one becomes such that it is impossible he should ever consent to turn himself from it [*thoroughly inept and a-potent manner of expressing the "Perfect," as weak as Rumi's and Bhagavad-Gita's*] for another sight; for the good, which is the object of the will, is all gathered in it, and outside of it that is defective which is perfect there. Now will my speech fall more short [*is he a sublime poet, he who has not the language to express sublimity but will* egotistically *proceed to do so?*], even in respect to that which I remember than that of an infant who still bathes his tongue at the breast [*in his egotism, Dante becomes obscene*]. Not because more than one semblance was in the Living Light [*don't think me a heretic for picturing the Trinity of Hinduism, or, is it really of Christianity*] wherein I was gazing, which ever is such as it was before; but through my sight, which was growing strong in me, as I looked, one sole appearance, even as I changed was altering itself to me. Within the profound and shining subsistence [*clichés*] of the lofty Light appeared to me three circles and one magnitude; and one seemed reflected by the other, as rainbow by rainbow [***outstanding** imagery*], and the third seemed fire breathed forth equally from the one and the other." Having studied Latin well, I know enough about the Italian language *as written*: we know this passage amounts to *only so much* in the original Italian verses,

Un punto solo m'è maggior letargo
 che venticinque secoli a la 'mpresa
 Nettuno ammirar l'ombra d'Argo.

Così la mente mia, tutta sospesa
mirava fissa, immobile e attenta,
e sempre di mirar faceasi accesa.

A quella luce cotal si diventa,
che volgersi da lei per altro aspetto
è impossibil che mai si consenta;

però che 'l ben, ch'è del volere obietto,
tutto s'accoglie in lei, e fuor di quella
è defettivo ciò ch'è li perfetto.

Omai sarà più corta mia favella,
pur a quel ch'io ricordo, che d'un fante
che bagni ancor la lingua a la mammella.

Non perché più ch'un semplice sembiante
fosse nel vivo lume ch'io mirava,
che tal è sempre qual s'era davante;

ma per la vista che s'avvalorava
in me guardando, una sola parvenza,
mutandom' io, a me si travagliava.

Ne la profonda e chiara sussistenza
de l'alto lume parvermi tre giri
di tre colori e d'una contenenza;

e l'un da l'altro come iri da iri
 parea reflesso, e 'l terzo parea foco
 che quinci e quindi igualmente si spiri.

Dante was a monk in his *intellect* but a gargantuan fantasist as an imaginative writer. Here he is in *Inferno* (Canto XXVI),

(translation by Singleton)

I was standing on the bridge, having risen up to see, so that if I had not laid hold of a rock I should have fallen below without a push; and my leader, who saw me so intent, said, "Within the fire are the spirits; each swathes himself with that which burns him."

"Master," I replied, "I am the more certain for hearing you, but already I thought it was so, and already I wanted to ask: who is that fire which comes so divided at its top that it seems to rise from the pyre where Eteocles was laid with his brother?"

He answered me, "Therewithin are tormented Ulysses and Diomedes, and they go together thus under the vengeance as once under the wrath; and in their flame they groan for the ambush of the horse which made the gate by which the noble seed of the Romans went forth **[trivial intellectually, but what majesty in the wording!: "groan for the ambush"]**; within it they lament the craft, because of which the dead Deidamia still mourns Achilles, and there for the Palladium they bear the penalty."

Dante gave his heart to only one little passage in his letter to Cangrande (where in his sharp turns from Beothius or Aristotle to "his own" ideas, it is clear that no normal scholar is attempting to write a normal thesis, but Dante himself, passing off as his own, false thoughts), a passage in it to which all the wretched editors and translators of Dante famous poem should have turned, and should in future turn, he states that the title of the poem is in full: "Begins the Comedy of Dante Alighieri, Florentine in birth, not in custom," and this line should be on the cover page of all versions of his book. The reader will remember that Dante, caught in exile, without any group to adhere to, called himself, "a party of one." *Begins the Comedy of Dante Alighieri, Florentine in birth, not in custom* has had, of course, like *Ulysses* and *The Odyssey*, countless imitators, the most tasteless and least original of whom is Goethe: Faust doubts, but Goethe wants very desperately to bring him to standardized religion, so as to make himself respected by the rabble, and therefore Goethe makes Margaret, the pure woman, be the vehicle of his redemption! And what a cloying *femme fatale*! — cloyingly perfumed, is Kinbote's phrase for women like her. And of course, Dostoevsky, with the *femme fatale* in *The Idiot* and *The Karamazov Brothers* who leads men to depravity and doom, and Sonya of *Crime and Punishment*, who leads the sinner to "redemption," but, of course, in the great Dostoevsky, fails, though selflessly following him to Siberia once the murder he has committed has been solved. Reading *Faust* in translation is much as I imagine reading *Ulysses* would be translated: one must *assume* the original is impeccably inked. Nietzsche's admiration of Goethe was primarily for Goethe's conversations with Eckermann, (filled with such passages of Goethe's shallow and pompous self-praise as,

We talked further about Voltaire, and Goethe recited to me his poem "Les Systèmes," from which I perceived how he must have studied and appropriated such things in early life.

He praised Gérard's translation as very successful, although mostly in prose.

"I do not like," he said, "to read my *Faust* any more in German, but in this French translation all seems again fresh, new, and spirited."

"*Faust*," continued he, "is, however, quite incommensurable, and all attempts to bring it nearer to the understanding are in vain. Also, it should be considered that the first part is the product of a somewhat dark state in the individual. However, this very darkness has a charm for men's minds, and they work upon it till they are tired, as upon all insoluble problems."

), not for *Faust*, which he excoriates in an earlier book, questioning, is *this* miserable development the *great* German *tragic* idea, as *scholars* have it, that Faust, with all his supernatural powers, cannot land Gretchen as a "piece of ass," this phrase in quotation being my cliché, not Nietzsche's wording (*Faust*. Send her another present. *Mephistopheles*. But——. *Faust*. I command you by the [*supernatural and silly*] authority I have over you.) ——Is this the best that Goethe and German literature can do outside Kafka, to whom I finally return? *I mean, simply, how can I put it more simply, does one need god's miracle of power over the devil to achieve this, to purchase a present for a young woman one is, for the nonce, infatuated with? Could not the "great scholar" Faust have gone to the best shop in his city and accomplish this without god's help?* Faust, that "incommensurable" work, is merely gigantically idealistic and false. Only Germans, who loved Wagner, Bismarck, and Hitler (not to mention Mann, Brecht, Wittgenstein, and Grass), could take this rubbish, *very stupid,* seriously.

An uneven writer, Kafka, who in the long story *In the Penal Settlement*, in the short tale "The Country Doctor", and in the very, very short story "On Parables" **[**

(translated by Willa and Edwin Muir)

"MANY complain that the words of the wise are always merely parables and of no use in daily life, which is the only life we have. When the sage says: "Go over," he does not mean that we should cross to some actual place, which we could do anyhow if the labor were worth it; he means some fabulous yonder, something unknown to us, something we cannot designate more precisely either, and therefore cannot help us here in the very least. All these parables really set out to say merely that the incomprehensible is incomprehensible, and we know that already. But the cares we have to struggle with every day: that is a different matter.

Considering this a man once said: Why such reluctance? If you only followed the parable you yourselves would become parables and with that rid of all your daily cares.

Another said: I bet that is also a parable.

The first said: You have won.
The second said: But unfortunately only in parable.
The first said: No, in reality: in parable you have lost." **]**

, is the composer of *the masterpieces of German writing, literary, philosophic, or political.*

Digression ended.

—, this passage, from Foucault's *Discipline, Punish*, I was saying, reads more like Kafka's *Penal Settlement* than like philosophy, as exemplified by Aristotle, and Aristotle's mortal foe, Hobbes,

"First, a strict spatial partitioning: the closing of the town and its outlying districts, a prohibition to leave the town on pain of death, the killing of all stray animals; the division of the town into distinct quarters, each governed by an intendant. Each street is placed under the authority of a syndic, who keeps it under surveillance; if he leaves the street, he will be condemned to death. On the appointed day, everyone is ordered to stay indoors: it is forbidden to leave on pain of death. The syndic himself comes to lock the door of each house from the outside; he takes the key with him and hands it over to the intendant of the quarter; the intendant keeps it until the end of the quarantine. Each family will have made its own provisions; but, for bread and wine, small wooden canals are set up between the street and the interior of the houses, thus allowing each person to receive his ration without communicating with the suppliers and other residents; meat, fish and herbs will be hoisted up into the houses with pulleys and baskets. If it is absolutely necessary to leave the house, it will be done in turn, avoiding any meeting. Only the intendants, syndics and

guards will move about the streets and also, between the infected houses, from one corpse to another, the 'crows', who can be left to die: these are 'people of little substance who carry the sick, bury the dead, clean and do many vile and abject offices'. It is a segmented, immobile, frozen space. Each individual is fixed in his place. And, if he moves, he does so at the risk of his life, contagion or punishment.

"Inspection functions ceaselessly. The gaze is alert everywhere: 'A considerable body of militia, commanded by good officers and men of substance', guards at the gates, at the town hall and in every quarter to ensure the prompt obedience of the people and the most absolute authority of the magistrates, 'as also to observe all disorder, theft and extortion'. At each of the town gates there will be an observation post; at the end of each street sentinels. Every day, the intendant visits the quarter in his charge, inquires whether the syndics have carried out their tasks, whether the inhabitants have anything to complain of; they 'observe their actions'. Every day, too, the syndic goes into the street for which he is responsible; stops before each house: gets all the inhabitants to appear at the windows (those who live overlooking the courtyard will be allocated a window looking onto the street at which no one but they may show themselves); he calls each of them by name; informs himself as to the state of each and every one of them 'in which respect the inhabitants will be compelled to speak the truth under pain of death'; if someone does not appear at the window, the syndic must ask why: 'In this way he will find out easily enough whether dead or sick are being concealed.' Everyone locked up in his cage, everyone at his window, answering to his name and showing himself when asked — it is the great review of the living and the dead...."

"This enclosed, segmented space, observed at every point, in which the individuals are inserted in a fixed place, in which the slightest

movements are supervised, in which all events are recorded, in which an uninterrupted work of writing links the centre and periphery, in which power is exercised without division, according to a continuous hierarchical figure, in which each individual is constantly located, examined and distributed among the living beings, the sick and the dead—all this constitutes a compact model of the disciplinary mechanism. The plague is met by order; its function is to sort out every possible confusion: that of the disease, which is transmitted when bodies are mixed together; that of the evil, which is increased when fear and death overcome prohibitions. It lays down for each individual his place, his body, his disease and his death, his well-being, by means of an omnipresent and omniscient power that subdivides itself in a regular, uninterrupted way even to the ultimate determination of the individual, of what characterizes him, of what belongs to him, of what happens to him. Against the plague, which is a mixture, discipline brings into play its power, which is one of analysis. A whole literary fiction of the festival grew up around the plague: suspended laws, lifted prohibitions, the frenzy of passing time, bodies mingling together without respect, individuals unmasked, abandoning their statutory identity and the figure under which they had been recognized, allowing a quite different truth to appear. But there was also a political dream of the plague, which was exactly its reverse: not the collective festival, but strict divisions; not laws transgressed, but the penetration of regulation into even the smallest details of everyday life through the mediation of the complete hierarchy that assured the capillary functioning of power; not masks that were put on and taken off, but the assignment to each individual of his 'true' name, his 'true' place, his 'true' body, his 'true' disease. The plague as a form, at once real and imaginary, of disorder had as its medical and political correlative discipline. Behind the disciplinary mechanisms can be read the haunting memory of 'contagions', of the plague, of rebellions, crimes, vagabondage, desertions, people who appear and disappear, live and die in disorder."

Both invert Proust and invert Foucault were, philosophically considered, *Idealists*, who *believed religiously* in impersonal elastic Time and anonymously recorded History, *respectively*; both Proust and Foucault were *aesthetes* (Foucualt's homosexual reveries inspire the passage, quite irrelevant to the narrative of the plague, *"A whole literary fiction of the festival grew up around the plague: suspended laws, lifted prohibitions, the frenzy of passing time, bodies mingling together without respect."* Foucault remembering the gay bars and the bathrooms of those bars where he "chatted" with male *strangers*, in America where he went to "teach") ruinously for their works, coming early in their lives into the delusion that they were *thinkers*, as they passed themselves off as, quite successfully, until this century. Foucault was too obtuse in not understanding the Idealism to where the logic of his arguments led.

As for ancient philosophy, on the state and on the "just" man, let us go to "the greatest literary master" among philosophers, Plato, and his *The Republic*. The *sickening* fact about Plato is how much he *lies* in his innumerable dialogues: *The Republic* (translated by Paul Shorey),
This, then, must be our conviction about the just man, that whether he fall into poverty or disease or any other supposed evil, for him all these things will finally prove good, both in life and in death. For the by gods assuredly that man will never be neglected who is willing and eager to be righteous, and by the practice of virtue to be like unto

God so far as that is possible for man.

It is reasonable, he said, that such a one should not be neglected by his like.

And must we not think the opposite of the unjust man?

Most emphatically.

Such then are the prizes of victory which the gods bestow upon the just.

So, I think, at any rate, he said.

But what, said I, does he receive from men? Is not this the case if we are now to present the reality? Do not your smart but wicked men fare as those racers do who run well from the scratch but not back from the turn? They bound nimbly away at the start, but in the end are laughed to scorn and run off the field uncrowned and with their ears on their shoulders. But the true runners when they have come to the goal receive the prizes and bear away the crown. Is not this the usual outcome for the just also, that toward the end of every action and association and of life as a whole they have honor and bear away the prizes from men?

So it is indeed.

Will you, then bear with me if I say of them all that you said of the unjust? For I am going to say that the just, when they become older, hold the offices in their own city if they choose, marry from what families they will, and give their children in marriage to what families they please, and everything that you said of the one I now repeat of the other, and in turn I will say of the unjust that most of them, even if they escaped detection in youth, at the end of their course are caught and derided, and their old age is made miserable by the contumelies of strangers and townsfolk. They are lashed and suffer all things which you truly said are unfit for ears polite. Suppose yourself to have from me a repetition of all that they suffer. But, as I say, consider whether you will bear with me.

Assuredly, he said, for what you say is just.

Such then while he lives are the prizes, the wages, and the gifts that the just man receives from gods and men in addition to those blessings which justice herself bestowed.

And right fair and abiding rewards, he said.

Well, these, I said, are nothing in number and magnitude compared with those that await both after death.

and so on.

Certainly, Plato would "bear with me" the comment that the man he considered the most just of all he had met, and of his age, Socrates, was certainly given high office and a fine wife—and never given the equivalent (or worse) of lashing, etc.—, *if he wished*, but wise men, do they wish for this?

Plato's, like all others' Idealism, is *wishful thinking*.

3

Political Philosophy

a

The Copernican break in philosophy comes, not with Descartes' epistemological declaration, "I think. Therefore, I am." Descartes is merely *rehashed Idealism*: the subject must exist before the object, *when the universe existed before life ever did*. Once Descartes is sure he *is* (see "Death and the Compass," by Borges), he starts to peer at the world and take it in.

Descartes' thought is not *true logically, as has been demonstrated above and will be below*. The break comes when Hobbes (my favorite philosopher) disputes with Aristotle himself, the "heathen" father of Christian and Moslem scholasticism. Both Hobbes and Aristotle are interested in the "truth." Aristotle is the first *encyclopedist*, Hobbes the *first* psychologist and *philosopher*. He singlehandedly created philosophy when none yet existed outside academic "brains."

Hobbes does away with Metaphysics, all, by *postulating* his own, obverse one, everything, including consciousness, is material, since it is occurring in the brain's motions. (Kant's elaborate epistemology and metaphysics, which he claimed were a "Copernican revolution," are entirely *redundant* after Hobbes.) Hobbes makes man like all other objects, Galilean.

In other words, he is saying to Descartes, figuratively but realistically, speaking, "Do we not from as early as we can make two-clause sentences using the word "I," already know that the physical head does the thinking?" This applies to blind people, too. Knowledge does not begin with "I think," because we always know that the physical head contains the hum of this activity. It is part of physical consciousness that it itself is felt to be occurring not in the chest or leg but in the head. Objectivity triumphs in Hobbes over subjectivity of fake idealism.

On the nature of man, Aristotle says, as his basis for both of his *Nicomachean Ethics* and his *Politics*, that man is a social animal.

Hobbes again disputes this. He says that man seeks to be alone *unless* he meets with another, and that when they meet they each *seek to extort the maximum admiration they can out of each other.*

Now, most people (i.e., academic philosophers) would say Aristotle came out triumphing over Hobbes (while backbiting each other with anxious competition, fawning, in the academic halls).

Let us see. The two (Aristotle was almost certainly Shakespeare's favorite philosopher (*Troilus and Cressida*, *The Taming of the Shrew*: Ulysses' quotation from Aristotle in the former is pure Hobbes, and a rarity in Aristotle: probably the dramatist's favorite philosopher would have been Hobbes, too, had Hobbes written before Shakespeare)) are saying the same thing. Hobbes' *manner* (or stylistic expression in the grand prose of the *Leviathan*, its only claim to *vulgar*, as opposed to this refined, glory: Hobbes' book, the part that matters, its FIRST PART: OF MAN, is not just about life being "brutish and short," as it has been made out to be, like Descartes' formulation, in the digital age) of saying does not contradict Aristotle. He merely adds to Aristotle's idea that man is social by nature, that he must interreact with other humans, for physical and mental sustenance (with which fact Hobbes has no quarrel since he knows that humans have always lived with each other, on friendly or inimical terms), the further one that we exclusively tend to extract maximum admiration out of all other people we meet and know, who are doing the same, when we meet each other, inevitably.

It is to agree with the social idea, and say, *psychologically* this "extraction" is *all* that is happening between people in *their smallest discursive and physical interactions with each other.*

This idea was the foundation of what can be called the subsequent pseudo-psychological philosophy that found its most ambitious expression in Helvétius' *Of the Mind*, according to one internet source the most widely read book in Europe of its time. Helvétius was to Hobbes what Kant was to Plato: the most *involved* and convoluted *academicizer* of the ideas of an earlier philosopher (himself an establisher of a school), and both shameless apists who do not name the earlier philosopher as the one whom they are stealing from: Helvétius names Locke as the Newton of philosophy, whom Montaigne and a few others anticipate in hints, but who gathered together and formalized philosophy for the first time, while filching from Hobbes' idea of the condition of nature and how man can leave it, putting the plagiarized part into a parenthesis in his book without acknowledgement; and Kant gives credit to Hume as the starting point of his quite patently Platonic "Critiques." What is unabashedly pleasure for Plato, passed off as truth, the world of Forms, is in Kant merely the Ideality which we can never know as experience, which begs the question: so, who cares what it is? From Kant came academics since, Hegel to Derrida to today; from Helvétius came out that utilitarianism which Dostoevsky mocked.

Stendhal, the finalizer of psychology, puts down the exact nature of what Hobbes means by those complicated words about extracting admiration. Stendhal calls it our *vanity*.

The Federalist Papers in America, and all related *earlier* matters, in the United States were all Hobbesian (not Lockean or Rousseauian) arguments, directed, more positively, not at legislation, but at the thinking through of a Constitution. Those writers in the new Republic were hammering out what structures to put in that would make Hobbesian humans *submit* (*islam* is the word for "submit" in classical Arabic) to those *structures* voluntarily and wish to prolong their existence, by birth or voluntarily ("but the Freudian … can still cast his vote, even if he is pleased to call it [*smiling*], political pollination." Shade to humble Kinbote). They thought about *everything* **practical** then, except for human ownership of human, and femininity. They thought enough so that no more thinking is done there

This much for philosophy, and I return to art.

Political Philosophy

b

a fantasy

Once I am widely read (i.e., long after my death: no gain in it for me) **PLEASE** *form political parties* in your respective countries, to overthrow democracy as a SYSTEM. Once "they" have won the will of the people, and have been "elected" to power, they should abolish their so-called "constitutions," choose by lot (i.e., lottery: "all life is coincidence," says Lola in Max Ophuls second and final masterpiece) their new queen, empress, emperor, or king. So, also, by lot, the dukes, duchesses, barons, baronesses, counts, countesses, marquises, etc., who, thus chosen *fairly* (unlike the corrupt system of camaraderies, finances, and advertised or speech-given *propaganda* of democracies today) are to *own* the equivalents in each country of what are called ridings in Canada, and districts in America. The rules of primogeniture should then be, different for each country, as becomes obvious from what follows, made by negotiations between new royalty and new aristocracy, etc. And they are to choose the minor nobility. All rule is to be through family lineage only (you can see what sacrifices to my principles I am making, by putting the sexual act at the center of politics again, when I *loathe* to my core, *sex*.) I am not advocating for the sort of activity that Trump the Bisony Duck (his throat, as proved Louis XVI's, even the guillotine blade cannot cut through in the first round, or even second round) will attempt in two or three years from now: that will be prompted by the desire to establish despotism in his *since-2001* (**January**), exactly speaking, doomed nation; what I am calling for is monarchy as defined by Montesquieu *in The Spirit of the Laws,* and further developed well (the best part of the book) by Helvétius in *De l'esprit:* the opposite of despotism, which they (both *very high aristocrats* of France (see the sort of garbage written by "political experts," commoners, in America and Britain today (such as good ol' "famous" "brave to death" Mr. Woodward))) detested as, brilliant minds as they were on this topic, leading to the sort of oppression that kills *culture.* The monarchical, which they associated with the system prevailing in *western Europe* then, which, they were not aware yet, produced Bach and Mozart, not the despotic, which is how they characterized *Asian* systems then.

Now, the argument presents itself, that *De l'esprit* itself was banned in France. This was not due to the monarch, though, but because *of the Roman Catholic Church,* despite its author's throwing in infrequently, in a half-hearted manner, phrases to the effect, "only Scripture can tell the full truth"; all religions and gods are *for this reason* to be banned in public. Whoever needs God ("No free man needs a God," John Shade says, in *Pale Fire*), is to keep his thoughts and worships to the confines of a personal home, and forbidden to propagandize to his or her children, *under penalty of death,* for 'tis a grave crime *to lie to one's own children,* for the sake of puffing up one's own *vanity*, when one has *no evidence* for his Arabian Night level religions.

Finally, on that argument, the book, despite the clerical ban, *was read by all educated Europeans* and, also, their *ungrateful* cousins-subjects, living in New World colonies, who rebelled with *fine-sounding* **lies** that covered up the barren *fact* that they wanted only to free themselves from taxes (money, the *sole* reason for the act of *treason* called the "Revolutionary" war—lust for wealth costumed as expression of equality of Negro and Madison): the proof is that they *transferred* power *only* to people **like themselves**, *propertied European-descent males*.

The very last piece of that argument, that posterity will have to decide on, since I myself know of no such texts, did western democracies allow the right to be, not only published, but *publicized*, of radical books?

I am not much interested in political reform for its own sake, though it is desperately needed in the declining world of today: merchants, capitalists, are to be the *slaves* of these families, their very lives and livelihoods dependent on the favor or wrath of king/queen, and local aristocrat.

Without such a change, once it is established throughout *most* of earth, culture, absolutely dead as lead right now, as I bear witness in 2018, unlike in Joyce's time, *will remain a corpse.*

Anyone who speaks or writes *publicly* of so-called freedom of the press (those of that profession should only record the acts of their masters, works of art—never to be "reviewed" by hacks: Picasso and Bergman could dupe thousands of such, but could not have *even one* of the patrons of Masaccio or the younger Rembrandt—, and local events such as murders, divorces, rebellions, treason, embezzlement, natural disasters, and so forth; journalists are to live with janitors, in co-inhabited residential buildings), so-called rights of the people (freedom of *thought* is to be preserved, but not of *expression*): *blasphemies against the religion called immaculate*, and public mentioning of "god" or "gods," like the other matters mentioned in *this* paragraph, are to be met with *beheadings* **on the spot,** by the royal or the ducal military or police, whose authority derives solely from the king or dukes, to whom *solely* are mandatory taxes to be paid, for the maintenance of the system.

You see, Masuda, Khrist, and Motoki are *freaks,* in every sense, and arose *against* possibilities within their democratic cultures: but only after several centuries of the reforms outlined, can a Titian or a Mozart appear. And *art and culture are the only excuses for societies to exist*: with artists (people such as myself) as servants of those aristocrats, too, rich, like Michelangelo, or penurious, like Bach.

What could the biological Shakespeare, born today, *possibly* do in those capitals of gaucheness and vulgarity, Broadway and Hollywood, or their equivalents in London or Milan or Bombay—certainly not compose *King Lear* or *Much Ado About Nothing*?

Either write plays about life in black ghettoes such as Harlem, or about Jewish Leopo heritage, as good old lacktalent Stoppard will in a few years, or about *lesbian* pimps—or about Mr. Alexander Hamilton, a non-entity.)

4

Literary biographies

"Early in 1914 James went to lunch with A.B. Walkley …
to meet Henry Bernstein. Bernstein talked to James of a new
writer named Marcel Proust and of his novel …, just
published. Edith Wharton later sent James a copy of the
book, but we do not know whether he read it or not."

From Leon Edel's one volume edition of his multi-
volume biography of Henry James.

And here, from George Painter's biography of Proust,

"London had received early news of *Swann* in an unsigned
review by A.B. Walkley…; he noticed the crucial
significance of the Two Ways, and compared *Swann*, as a
study of a child's contact with a corrupt adult world, to
Henry James' *A Small Boy* and *What Maisie Knew*. Perhaps the
Master felt urged to read *Swann* for himself after seeing this
article. He obtained a copy early in 1914 from his friend
Edith Wharton, the distinguished American novelist in
Paris, and was discovered immersed in it by Logan Pearsall
Smith. 'His letter to me showed how deeply it had impressed
him,' wrote Mrs. Wharton, 'he seized upon *Swann* and
devoured it in a passion of curiosity and admiration … he
recognized a new mastery, a new vision….' He wrote Proust
a magnificent letter, informing him that this was an
extraordinary book for so young an author (Proust was then

forty-two, and James seventy), and that it was a great pity that he lived in advance of his time. *Du Côté de chez Swann* was the greatest French novel since *La Chartreuse de Parme*, he truly declared, but perhaps (and here James was fortunately in error), Proust would suffer the fate of Stendhal and not be recognized in his lifetime."

Whom to believe, Edel or Painter? Henry James thought that *The Red and the Black* was "un-readable," but that *The Charterhouse of Parma* was a very fine novel, with this caveat that it should only be read by those "morally" formed and educated, and so would not be corrupted by *The Charterhouse of Parma*'s thought and morals. These comments are from pieces James himself published in his lifetime. He *greatly* preferred Balzac (whom he considered as the greatest of all novelists in history so far) to Stendhal, and Balzac wrote many of his most celebrated novels *after* the publication of *The Charterhouse of Parma.*

And here are two egregious bits of invention of psychological states of the subject being written of, by the biographer, both from Richard Ellman's *James Joyce: New and Revised Edition.*

"In general [Joyce] had lost interest in his earlier book, *Finnegans Wake* have pre-empted its position, but he allowed himself one day to ask Beckett, 'Does anyone in Dublin read *Ulysses?*' 'Yes' said Beckett. 'Who?' Beckett named some names. 'But they are all Jews.' Joyce said. Beckett mentioned then that many intellectuals were turning now to Kafka. The name was known to Joyce only as that of the sinister translator of the *Franfurter Zeitung*, Irene Kafka, and he was perplexed and bothered by this new aspirant to literary pre-eminence."

That conversation bit may have been reported to Ellman, the biographer, but the rest is just *bosh* invented out of Ellman's own egotism at imagining himself being outdone by some other biographer of Joyce, Yeats, Wilde, and other *only Irishmen.*

"It was impossible to remain unknown for long. Joyce went into a bookshop in the *Politiken* building, and ordered a book to be sent to his hotel. The bookseller at once recognized his name, and showed him that *Ulysses* was on sale there, news which pleased Joyce as much as the information that *Lady Chatterley's Lover* had sold more copies displeased him."
Doctor Richard Ellman Freud-Jung, again at it.

'Tis a pity that the author who had composed the delightful and endlessly re-readable *Ulysses* should have taken the route of *Finnegans Wake* next, not because the latter is a bad book (Joyce reading from the "ALP" section of in one of his only two audio recordings—the other is his reading from the newspaper office chapter in *Ulysses*—shows in an incontradictable manner how beautifully *musical* his prose in *Finnegans Wake* is—perhaps he should have made an audio recording of the *entire text* as soon as the book was published—which occurred right before Hitler invaded France and forced Joyce to flee to Switzerland, where he died a few years later and is buried, in the same land as are his only two rivals in twentieth-century letters, Borges and Nabokov—, for it seems that *Finnegans Wake* is an aural book, one meant for the ear, and not for the eye and the mind, so that it belongs more with Masuda, Debussy, and Mozart, than with *Ulysses* and *Paradise Lost*), but because it is impenetrable, and I have read no more than thirty pages of its beginning, and the famous "Anna Livia Plurabelle" section, without understanding a *word* of *either* part.

Perhaps for this reason, we discovered once, when we were touring India, Bangladesh, Pakistan, and Sri Lanka during a summer vacations break, that a British Council Library (an official institution of the U.K. government), in a branch located in the capital city of one of those countries, possessed a copy of *Finnegans Wake*—since its "obscenities" could not be understood by anyone—, but no copy of *Ulysses*—checked out, or on the shelf—because *Ulysses* contains sentences such as the following, from the beginning of one of the scenes in it,

"Pineapple rock, lemon platt, butter scotch. A sugarsticky girl shovelling scoopfuls of creams for a christian brother. Some school treat. Bad for their tummies. Lozenge and comfit manufacturer to His Majesty the King. God. Save. Our. Sitting on his throne sucking red jujubes white.

Petty-minded descendants of Shakespeare *have never forgiven* the Irish *colonized-born* Joyce for writing of them like this, and doing so in more beautiful and intelligent English-language than any Englishman or Englishwoman has ever written, *except for Shakespeare.*

Thou art a monument without a tomb,
And art alive still while thy book doth live
And we have wits to read and praise to give.

III

1

Masuda: Music

1976-1981 was the period of *fame* for Masuda Keiko, of the Japanese band, Pink Lady.

    #1 in her time, what Masuda sought is the opportunity *to express*, with voice, dance, and face—Dwight Macdonald, the American *socialist* "intellectual," in the 1960's (or was it near his death in the 1970's?), pointed out the fatal flaw of cinema (which he should have extended to music) as an art form: that the type of fame it produces corrupted artists who were "interesting" to begin with, but became **insufferable** *after fame*: I think he was speaking of the theme of Fellini's *8½* (which he should have applied to the fashionable use of Jung by the already long-successful and long-praised Fellini, rather than to promote that film's supposed "greatness": *8½* seems to be filled with "great" shots utterly unconnected in any intellectual or philosophic basis with each other, and many pointless ones, such as the zooming in and out of the camera on the dead father's face in the protagonist's dream-vision near the beginning: "Who was that 'nymph' I saw?" in a vision at a holy water distribution sight, thinks the hero on the voiceover—she turns out to be, in "reality," *merely* a starlet who gives him advice on his upcoming project, later in the picture!), and he used a few examples, of which I remember only Hitchcock, but it can be applied to Dreyer, to Bergman, to Fritz Lang, to Sternberg, to Antonioni, to Tarkovsky, and virtually everyone else in cinema of the artsy popular brand, except Kurosawa, Hawks, and Ozu: it can be applied to nearly all figures of classical and modern music, except Johann Sebastian Bach: after all, Mozart called one of his symphonies *Prague*, and another, *Linz*, *because he was popularly accoladed there*, in eastern Austro-Hungary, as he was never in *adulthood* in Vienna, and wished to please and *flatter his flatterers*: and Beethoven arrogantly told a humble admirer who said he could not "understand" the trashy and empty "*Appassionata*" piano sonata, "It is not written for you, but for posterity"!!!—but the same does *not* apply to Masuda, who, in disc 2 of the Fuji television "The Night's Hit Studio" show's DVD, is to be seen in *very high spirits* one night *before* her *final* Pink Lady retirement concert of 1981—(after which, she was clear-headed enough to know, she would lose almost all fame, and did, except for the temporary solo hit, "Sparrow" later in 1981, and then nothing along the celebrity line)—, *the exact date of the broadcast* was March 30, 1981—[*see which*; I want to compare verse 223 of Surah 2 of the notoriously criminal *Quran*, authored by the Shingenian *villain*, Muhammad, to the equally evil *Bible* where, in the story of Jephthah, bible, Judges, chapter 11-12 (*also invoked by the "believing" Shakespeare*, when Hamlet once encounters Polonius, that *subtle* storyteller of a playwright being quite conscious of bible's criminal nature, psychology, and *intent*); the said Jephthah promises an imaginary Yahweh (who never existed outside the *sick* Jewish mind) that were he to prevail in the upcoming battles, he will sacrifice to

Yahweh the first being he sees when he returns home, only to find his sole beloved daughter greeting him there, whom *he, with "Woe is me" cries, gladly SLAUGHTERS, in return* for Yahweh's granting *his political ambition's dream realization*!!!], one day before the enforced-by-Victor Entertainment's executives' FINAL CONCERT OF PINK LADY of March 31, 1981, when Masuda *could have guessed that the glitter and glamor of fame were going to vanish forever from her life*)—on the occasion where the hosts of that Fuji show present her, and her band partner Nemoto, with a basket of delicacies of *raw* plants that they claim are very delicious to eat: Masuda is positively "*giggling*" at the moment *when she recognizes* the contents of that basket.

She went on, in post-Pink Lady years, to produce supreme masterpieces, "*Suzume*" ("Sparrow"), "It's Mt. Fuji", and the just released "*Del Sole*," while Nemoto, also continuing her career as singer, accomplished, by herself of value, *nothing*.

Her art is audiovisual, and not limited to the musical, even more as regards her face than her *exquisitely* dancing body during a song.

That Masuda has to rely on *the camera* for maximum musical impact is not, perhaps, all that different from composers relying on a *conductor*: the *full* impact of Mozart and Beethoven, so far, has only been heard when they were conducted by Georg Solti, *by far* the greatest conductor, not excluding Toscanini and Karajan (the latter invariably has the music played too rapidly, trying to effect a *dramatic* hoppity effect, without succeeding), since recordings began: Beethoven's symphonies, Mozart's greatest masterpieces, Symphony No. 40 and *Le Nozze di*

Figaro (the orchestration of it), all of them, I have never *heard* the full beauty, hidden from me by my inability to read musical notes *fluently* (after all, after a certain age, Beethoven could only "hear," by reading music, and it was thus that he, for himself, at least, replaced *in his esteem* Mozart with Handel as the greatest master of musical composition in history so far), except in Solti's versions.

So, with the camera and Masuda, the complete manifestation of what *this superlative genius* wished to express, and does express.

In an exact sense, the cognoscenti of true music should learn the musical notation system and *read* Bach (who hardly ever probably heard his music played more than once per piece, if that), Handel, Mozart (who was hardly performed in Vienna), Beethoven (deaf by the time he *wrote* his major work), and Schubert (his best, the so-called *Unfinished Symphony*, did he ever hear it performed by a full orchestra?). And the cognoscenti should seehear Masuda. Quite simple, really, for Mozart etc. *wrote* and Masuda *performs*.

One fact that is constant in great music: the words that are used in vocal music are of little to no importance: this applies to the conventional words of Bach's cantatas, to Mozart's *Mass in C minor*, to the already conventional-by-then sentiments of "man's fraternity with other men" of Schiller's "Ode to Joy," to which Beethoven provided the music in the last movement of his *Ninth* symphony, and to the lyrics of Masuda's songs, where they are of infinitely little significance. Words *only* matter in music, when music is simple and *trite*, and one forms a sentimental attachment to the inevitably sentimental words of a song.

Stendhal wrote for posthumous consumption, in *The Life of Henri Brulard*, that the French are incapable of composing music (yes, he is even "supposed" to have not ruled out having based Julien on Berlioz—the very thought!), and that France had only produced one great work in that medium, the *Marseillaise*.

America and Canada, so far as I know of the latter, have no music: the only "effective" one, in double quotes, is the "Cutthroat" tune in Hawks' *Rio Bravo* (a purely artistic picture: Hawks, unfortunately, would mix high art with mere entertainment, either because he could not tell the difference, or because he was the product of a purely commercial society/nation—even *Bringing Up Baby*, which should have been pure art, is mixed; only his own *Rio Bravo* (great art is characterized by *true thought*: Carlos, the Hispanic hotel owner, is a man whose intelligence the white sheriff respects as much as he respects his white friends; and, *in fact*, is shown to be far more sensible than that sheriff's good buddy, Pat; as Shakespeare with the "negro," Othello; or Rembrandt, in his painting of two African men brought to Netherlands, there is no thought that a man of a different race will not have the sensitivity of the artist's own race; on the other hand, look at the *utter* "*horror*" implied (?, no, made the central theme of the movie), an "Injun" man *touching the body* of a "pure, white" woman in Ford's asinine and wretchedly directed, visually, *The Searchers*, a young woman who has to be *forgiven* by whites and a racially mixed young man at the end, and taken in, the "nobility" of these latter implied in *their* generosity toward a *despoiled* fellow white woman (played by Natalie Wood)—Kant *opposed* miscegenation on what he purported were *solidly philosophic* grounds!—: in an episode of his tv show, Dean Martin, hosting John Wayne, whose own favorite of his own performances was the one in *The Searchers*, discusses with Wayne, *Rio Bravo*, both actors speaking as if it were any **regular** "western" genre film they had co-acted in!—certainly, *only Hawks* was the true artist involved in that picture, everyone else his artistic slaves, *who were encouraged by him* to ad-lib, whenever they had a good notion) and Keaton's *Sherlock Jr.* escape this problem (and a work in another art medium, Jacob Lawrence's painting *Blind Beggars* (1938), probably the greatest painting of the twentieth century (at the Met Museum online site is given, under a digital image of the work, the following line about it "Due to rights restrictions, this image cannot be enlarged, viewed at full screen, or downloaded." The truly *hilarious* fact is that the Met also notes "Not on view": one cannot see the original of the greatest painting of its century because the "museum" staff think…. —Ah curators! you have *indeed* always been blessed by the Father with *minds*: Hopper's mediocre *Nighthawks* (if a *diner* scene can be art, it is in Hawks' *The Big Sleep*: *just watch it*: *starting* from it, the major work of Hawks, after *Rio Bravo*) is, I am sure, "on view"), *if* one takes Monet to be only a nineteenth century artist) (while Dickens, in his middle period, at least, in *Bleak House* and *Little Dorrit*, could *effortlessly* combine entertainment and art, as had Pope in the previous century, in *The Dunciad* and *The Rape of the Lock* (Keats, in his best lyrics, odes, sonnets, *Lamia*, and *The Eve of St. Agnes*, Coleridge (no Coleridge: no Poe, as poet; no Shakespearean tragedies, Milton, and KJV version of Old Testament combination: no Blake, no Melville, no Faulkner—and, so, also, outside English, no García

Márquez, best *artist* (*One Hundred Years of Solitude, Chronicle of a Death Foretold,* first half of the first chapter of *Love in the Time of Cholera, extremely* fine minor masterpieces, like the stories of Chekhov and of the early Hemingway) not merely writer, of *his* generation—Tarkovsky, Foucault, Pynchon, Claude Simon, Truffaut, Godard, Grass, Mailer, Fassbinder, Wajda, etc., etc.—, who combined that strain with the best Spanish tradition to date before himself, outside of Velázquez (*The Triumph of Bacchus,* 1628-1629,

)

and Goya, the *elements of fantasy*, Cervantes-Borges) in "Kublai Khan" and *The Rime of the Ancient Mariner*, and Austen, in *Pride and Prejudice* and *Persuasion*, rose even higher: their *art* **is** *entertaining*, as *Rio Bravo* is: *Chance*. "Let's take a turn around the town; and also bring some coffee for Stumpy," (Stumpy is introduced into the film, for the first time, with equal exquisiteness; *and* at the climax: *Chance*. "Good ol' Stumpy, the fella I left behind.") the "turn" Chance and Dude then take: *crystal-faceted* art), the American artist of ambition, for either of the reasons given above regarding Hawks, goes generally for the excessively *unentertaining*, hoping thereby to convince his or her audience that "art" is being attempted, Emerson, Hawthorne, Thoreau, Melville, Dickinson, Henry James, Crane, Dreiser, Eliot, Pound, Frost, Faulkner, O'Neill, Tennessee Williams, Welles, Ellison, Copland, Dylan, Springsteen, Pollock, Wyeth, de Kooning, Kubrick, Bellow, Pynchon, Streep, D. Hoffman *(Mon père et mon oncle maternel ont beaucoup admiré* Kramer vs. Kramer, *en 1981. Le premier, sincère, a dit que l'actrice avait encore mieux joué que le bel acteur. Le second s'est exclamé : "Quelle perspicacité! C'est ce que disent aussi les critiques américains."*), or becomes a sub-artistic entertainer, Irving, Fenimore Cooper, Poe, Whitman, Twain, Hemingway, Groucho Marx, John Ford, Updike, Gershwin, Presley, Madonna, Rockwell, Warhol, Coppola, Scorsese, T. Morrison, J. Nicholson: the *same*, with less **international** *fame*, with Canadians: the Munro-Atwood "artist," and the Neil Young-Justin Bieber "entertainer") the masterpieces, no doubt, of American cinema; not equaled in American literature, even by Melville and Faulkner, except in one work, by a "foreigner," titled *Pale Fire*: on this topic, the masterpiece of all French cinema, style without content, as in Chateaubriand, for no woman can change, or be, as the heroine in it does, or is—I thought the transformation was "realistic" when I was eighteen, and so made the most ridiculous mistakes in my dealings with "real women," when *all* women *except* Masuda and Motoki (and, of course, the reader; if it happens to be a male, except his mother and his mate) are mentally flabby—, is the entire final embassy ball scene of Ophuls' *Madame de*, starting with the dance chart being signed by Donati, to the General's and his wife, the Countess, Madame de's, walking down the majestic staircase, as they leave the ball: virtuosic *and* ravishing: if Ophuls had managed to make the entire picture as audiovisually rich as that extended scene (there are some longish moments, in the circus ring scenes, in his *Lola Montès*, that rise to that level, also: Lola *not* reaching out with her arm toward the ringmaster as he extends his, while her successes with Russians are being spoken of by him, as she glides across the circus grounds, for example), why, then, we would have had a *true* equal in cinema, outside of Kurosawa, to *Youjinbou* and *The Hidden Fortress!*—both Ophuls and Hawks worked in very friendly manners with their actors and actresses (Danielle Darrieux, who played Madame de, and others, in Ophuls' pictures, remembered, in an interview in the 2000's, "Before a shoot he would rarely speak of the scene; he would talk of other things, and, as I was performing my part, I would remember what he had just said, and would understand what to do in the scene."), to get excellent performances from them: Kurosawa was ruefully known on his sets as the "Emperor," for the extreme demands that his perfectionism led him to make on every member of the filming team, even with close friends among actors: Donald Richie, the American historian of Japanese cinema, recalled an event during the shooting of *The Hidden Fortress*: while he was directing, Kurosawa was paying great attention to his pen, which had stopped working: instead of obtaining a new one, he persistently worked on the old, twisting it, hitting it, hammering, etc., until finally, by the end of that day's shooting, he had fixed it: that night, as Richie, Mifune, and some others on the set, were relaxing together, in a hot communal bath, someone mentioned Kurosawa's pen-manhandling of that day, etc., and Mifune, who was playing in the picture the role of Makabe Rokurota, the samurai general of the defeated party, said, "I, too, feel like that pen."), the *El Degüello*, composed by Dimitri Tiomkin, to suit Hawks' high theme in the film.

"Indigenous" North American music are jazz, rock, and rap: they all come out of African tradition, and like Latin America's and Caribbean's, need animal-muscle instincts, good for public dances of primitive orgy attractions, not for the spirit isolated. They should be targeted to the rabble (see the quotation from Foucault much above: peasants revelling and dancing in an orgy (one knows *very* well what they used to *look* like: there are several *immortal* depictions of them, by Peter Paul Rubens) where normal restrictions of society have been lifted, including the post-Classical, christian, banning of homosexuality, I suppose, for *him*). Ideal.

Now, Masuda gave gargantuan concerts. I have seen two, on dvd recordings. The concerts are not of much importance, artistically. It is in the live performances on *contemporary* television *shows*, over the decades, where Masuda's art is evidenced.

2

Motoki: Acting

Cinema Surpassing

Dwight MacDonald, probably the finest of *all* twentieth-century film critics, not merely American, wrote an essay apart from all others, in a 1970's book, *Favorite Movies*, with contributions of an essay each by critics as wide-ranging as Stanley Kauffmann (*Tokyo Story*), Molly Haskell (*Madame de*), Richard Roud (*The Rules of the Game*), Richard Corliss (*French Can Can*), John Simon (mostly Bergman's such as *Persona, Sawdust and Tinsel, Smiles of a Summer Knight*, though, I paraphrase from memory, "the same level is reached in a few Antonioni's, Fellini's *The White Sheikh* and *I Vitelloni*, and, perhaps, by some Japanese directors, whose language I do not have any knowledge of, and so cannot fully judge." Around the same time, but I do not remember which year—I am writing this in the attic of my mansion, since my wife and I quarreled today over the choices and prices of a kitchen-do-over, and I have been exiled from the matrimonial bed—, he wrote an entire book on Bergman, but this must have been after Picasso and Stravinsky died, because he, who kept up a very carefully and consciously sought reputation of being *super* "high-brow" about *all* the arts, would have had to wait until then, and could, afterwards, safely ignore Kurosawa and Borges, when he asked Bergman in the introductory interview, published with his analyses of the four or five films discussed in that book, like a thrilled young girl being introduced to Ringo Starr, "How does it feel to be the greatest artist, in the greatest art medium, of your age?" What an *austerely* high-brow mind, one cannot help exclaiming!), and others of the English-speaking world, holding forth on *their* favorite picture(s).

Though I, a film critic of the 1990's, who obtained his first break in an L.A. newspaper film column in 1987, and have since become one of those always quoted in advertisements by producers, rarely agree with MacDonald, I always find his arguments for and against particular films arresting, *cogent*, and worth considering.

He named *8½* as his favorite film, because, for him, it was visually richer, in its kaleidoscopic manner, than any film since *Citizen Kane*. But, and here we get to the interesting part, he said he liked many pictures, and listed all the ones he liked in chronological order, putting an asterisk sign before the ones he particularly admired or loved.

I don't have his essay in front of me, but I *do* remember that *some* of the asterisk ones were (with often, runner up listed by the same director),

The Birth of a Nation (runner up, *Intolerance*)
Ten Days that Shook the World (runner up, *Battleship Potemkin*)
Sherlock Jr. (runner up, *The General*)
The Grand Illusion (runner up, *The Rules of the Game*)
Trouble in Paradise (I can't remember the runner up, by Lubitsch)
Citizen Kane (runner up, *The Magnificent Ambersons*)

Children of Paradise (I don't recall whether he had another Carné)

Rashomon (runner up, either *The Seven Samurai* or a very little-known Kurosawa that I haven't seen)

La Ronde (no runner up by Ophuls)

Tokyo Story (no runner up by Ozu)

Sawdust and Tinsel (runner up, *Wild Strawberries*) [perhaps other way around]

L'avventura (with, if I remember correctly, Antonioni's first film as runner up, *Le Amiche*)

8½ (with runner up a film I saw only ten minutes of, before getting so bored by Fellini that I stopped watching it—with his wife as protagonist, of the late 1950's)

Though I myself greatly prefer *Late Spring* to *Tokyo Story* of Ozu, and *To Be or Not To Be*, or even the *first* half of *Ninotchka*, to *Trouble in Paradise* among Lubitsches, I find that list to be fascinatingly interesting as a compendium of *first-rate* twentieth-century tastes (we are about to get away from that century).

Since he has "done the job" for directors so admirably, that is, he has all the best directors (if one includes the total list), I will do my little bit.

ALL of cinema from 1894 or 1895 through this day, the last of 1996, has been TRASH. I myself have made much money and reputation from my talent at coining bubbly, positive "quotable quotes" for garbage such as *The Age of Innocence* ("dazzlingly colored kaleidoscopic miracle") that were enthusiastically embraced by the Industry, those manufacturers of toilets, of which I am a distinguished propagandist.

Since I am very desirous to keep my fortune and name brilliant, and to be invited to the Academy Awards and Globe Awards, etc. ceremonies—I wanted to starve as Beckett did, but had no literary talent, not even a trace of it, so I am now a multi-multi-millionaire. I like being invited to Stephen Sp.'s parties, and kid around with Brad.

That is to say, I *despise to the core of my soul everything filmic*, but need to lead a luxurious life, a man without natural gifts. Therefore, I instruct my lawyer, and good friend, to publish this as my farewell-to-the-Industry article on the newly invented method of communication, called the world wide web, *within one hour*, I repeat, *1 hour* after the very public I am pronounced dead by doctors and authorities. Journalists and bloggers can write my obituary the next day.

My motive is that I am a *very* handsomely remunerated *sweatshop laborer*, and have always been consumed by a desire to commit suicide, but *only when I am doing my job*, **seeing modern and classic movies**. My real writing (will I be classed with Beckett?), only here, is but a note from where I will be, when it is first read, even by my lawyer, since this will be given to him sealed, underground.

My respected elder, Mr. Rogero Guiterrez-Eberto, wrote in a paid article for *Video Review* magazine around 1986-1987 that here were his fave faves of all time, including such gems as Werner Herzog's *Aguirre: The Wrath of God* (a tasteless imitation-adaptation, unacknowledged, of Conrad's *Heart of Darkness*, set in the New World, with a Spanish legendary character of history and the Amazon jungle as the supposed backdrops: I think Mr. Eberto may have had a Coppola, too, don't remember, was it *Apocalypse Now*, an adaption, again, acknowledged, of the Conrad novella?: Welles wanted to adapt that novella before changing topic *at the last moment* to a fictionalized biopic of the newspaper tycoon, William Randolph Hearst, *Citizen Kane*) and Martin Scorsese's *Taxi Driver* which he called "the *Crime and Punishment* of cinema," the protagonist's calisthenics with straps-on and a handgun + the pails of red paint *gently hosed* and *hoisted* on to *defenseless* walls at the end to signify bloody death: *psychology*!

My own analogy to *Crime and Punishment*-level psychology (not the inferior *The Idiot* level of psychology, where Dostoevsky made the central character one he wants us to emulate, the meek, christ-like Prince Myshkin (the great Russian is always honest *in his major **fiction***: to be **chirst-like in this world**, one has to be sub-par intellectually and emotionally, a retard, *an idiot*: a man with a full brain could never *descend* to that level: Dostoevsky lies only in discursive prose, but, again, he himself wrote, either in a letter to a friend that has survived, or in his *A Writer's Diary*, I paraphrase, "I cannot write philosophy straight out; I have to dramatize and put in into a novel's form to express what I think," or words to that effect); but *Crime*'s, where he made a character he does not wish us to be like, a nihilist) is the actress Motoki Noriko, who, at the age of sixteen, is on that level, as for example, in the second episode of the work of all the episodes she appears in, the 1974-1975 Japanese television science fiction series *Denjin Zaboga* ("Electroman Zaboga"), where, when the boy in love with her girl-character, Ken, advises her to return to her deceased father's residence, against the wishes of the *non-amorously inclined* hero, Däimon, in the close-up of Motoki, which by script standards is supposed to *show her undetermined or thinking over* of the alternatives, she expresses in her eyes, *both* a certain hesitant sympathy, and a *deep loathing* of Ken, whom she is looking at, in the scenario.

But Motoki goes further than Dostoevsky: at times (for example, the entirety of her acting in episode 50, she is meek, quite, docile—except in that one expression of twisted suffering, right after Zaboga base has been blown up, and there is a panning close-up shot of Ken, Yuki (her character), the child Hiroshi, and the hero, Däimon): she accomplishes the equivalent of forcing the combination of Raskolnikovian nihilism and Myshkinian simplicity into one character, veering from one to the other, to express a fully developed philosophic vision, rather than a unified character, what Dostoevsky could not imaginatively force through in a single novel: he has to divide the dual visions into two separate novels, and cannot reconcile them until an *unresolved* bipartite division in *The Karamazov Brothers* in its most profound scenes, those between the grooming-to-be-an-Orthodox priest, Alyosha, and his skeptic brother, Ivan.

But I doubt Mr. Eberto, Mr. Simon (who thinks that the man who portrayed Patton in the film of that name, and Frederick March, who sexually harassed Carole Lombard on the sets of *Nothing Sacred*, are *by far* the greatest of all actors, male and female, since recordings began), and the late Mr. MacDonald understood *anything* regarding psychology in acting.

If we substitute "Motoki" for "Shakespeare" and "Lord Bacon," "art" for "reading," and "Yuki" for "Hamlet," the following passage, from Nietzsche's Ecce Homo, *becomes more fully true,*

"*I know of no more heart-rending reading than Shakespeare: what a man must have suffered to have such a need of being a buffoon!*

"*Is Hamlet understood? Not doubt, but* certainty *is what drives him insane.—But one must be profound, an abyss, a philosopher to feel that way.—We are all* afraid *of truth.*"

Now, after making the clichéd comment that Bacon was the originator of the plays, Nietzsche goes on, with philosophy, **not speculation**,

"*We are very far from knowing enough about Lord Bacon, the first realist in every sense of the word, to know everything he did, wanted, and experienced in himself.*"

3

Absurdities: Gods and Godless *Nibbana*

Sikhs regard the *comb* as the highest creation of human history.

Secondly, they value *discipleship* to the Gurus. Like the Judaic prophets, like Jesus, like Buddha, like Confucius, like etc., the *original* Gurus, starting with the originator of this *sect*, Guru Nanak, are the *sole sources* of Truth. Mankind is left to these Guru's version of Truth, which has to be solemnly obeyed at all costs. See the later passage in this chapter, the notion about God possessing values different from humans'—**the** *sole* **reason why this disease, religion, can, psychologically speaking, exist in humans**, "wise" or "fools" alike. Here is a passage from the central sacred Sikh "scripture," the *Adi Granth*, (Majh: mahala III, section XI)

"I am devoted O Lord, I devoted [to those who] apply their minds to Hari. The true Hari is obtained by attachment to the Guru, (who) is easily causing him [Hari] to dwell in the heart. If he (i.e., the disciple) serve the true Guru, then he obtains everything. He obtains such a fruit as he is desiring. The true Guru is the giver of all things, by a perfect destiny that he is obtained. The (human) mind is dirty, and does not meditate on the One." Etc., etc.

This is *essentially no different* from, "Follow Allah *and* His Prophet," "Follow Socrates and Plato," "Follow the Father *and* His Son," "Follow the Awakened One [Buddha]," "Follow the Leader [*Il Duce*] Mussolini," etc., etc.: it is the *same* trite formula, which is *political* at its base, to gain power over the masses.

O God, your claim that there is an afterlife, how can we trust it after you give us a brain, and using it *as* we did to discover You, we as humans have perversely discovered through human investigations that *consciousness* and *all* its mode and mood and nature are wholly determined by the physiology of the quite demonstrably perishable brain, blood rushing through a mealy, pink drizzle? Surely, you could have helped us more here. Why never define the exact nature of what it is to be a thinking *soul*? *What* is the soul, and why has it been universally in all cultures thought to exist, if it be a common illusion? O Atma, tell us! Scientists tell us that it arises from synapses, but this is like explaining *subjective* delight of painted *sight* by describing *light*. Why were humans evolutionarily not made to have an eye for radio waves, rather than light? O atma-imbued scientist, tell us!

God's claim, *implicit* in the Bible, the Vedas, and Bhagavad-Gita, the Adi Granth, *explicit* in the Quran, is, ever, plaintively, bring forth a passage of words comparable to this that I inspire....

Abraham, Muhammad, Jeanne d'Arc.

An old edition of the *Britannica* triumphantly suggested that Jesus is different from all other religious founders in not being an ecstatic: he was in his "own right mind" when he would "talk" to the imaginary Father.

By this standard Saul called Paul, without whom, everyone admits, Jesus would have been forgotten, was an ecstatic.

Some madmen and madwomen are considered by the rabble to be most sacred and scary personages in *metaphysics*. Others are locked up. If one is insane she or he is either looked up to or locked up.

Buddha claimed to remember the *details* of his past lives, and fought against a very physically "real" demon Mara, like Jesus in the wilderness.

I prefer the great writer Tsuji Masaki's anime character Devilman, *Debiruman*, who is able to slay evil God in the final episode, out of love *for a human being.*

Ramayana, the Sanskrit epic *poem* (certainly superior to the trash forced upon English- or German-speaking students by their *kind* educational institutions, which now teach only so-called "theory," such as *The Canterbury Tales—Beowulf* in Old English is far more effective than this *gas* of Middle English (Chaucer, with his tale about *farting* in it, would not have been offended by this insult), another Middle English trash poem, called, I think, *Pearl*, which I was *supposed* by *my* professor in college to have been forced-read, as I was supposed to have read, also, the entire TCT of Chaucer, in graduate school: I have a singular gift of being able to write long essays on a book that I have read only a few pages of the beginning, the middle, and the end of—or *Faust*) is by one of the largest consciousness of ancient times (we regard the modern age to have begun in Europe; with Giotto and Dante in the arts, with Copernicus in the sciences, with Hobbes in psychology, Spinoza in religious thought (not for *Ethics*, but for *Theological-Political Treatise*), and Locke in political thought), Valmiki, that dwarfs even Taj Mahal, the Parthenon of India, and Kalidasa, the Tasso of India— very well translated into English by a man named Nash, a professor in his time, and of whom, Tasso, after another fragment, Stendhal writes in one of the "Fragments" section of his treatise, *Of Love*, (I quote from memory), "This fact makes me amused by those who consider Homer superior to Tasso. Crystallization existed in ancient Greece, and not far from Homer.").

Ramayana is treated as Hindu scripture by believing Hindus, though it is not a part of the Vedas, and is regarded by many of them as their holiest text—since Hindus have many holy days, but the holiest and *most observed* is Diwali, which celebrates Rāma's return in the company of his half-brother, and his formerly kidnapped wife, Sita, whose rescue forms the main string-knot of the epic's plot, to his kingdom; among Hindi speaking Hindus, at least, the most common form of greeting, used both in meeting and parting are *namaste* ("bowing") and *namaskar* (the same meaning); the only one where the name of a "god" is used, commonly or rarely, as far as we have encountered, is "Ram Ram," Ram being the Hindi version of the Sanskrit name Rāma: though Valmiki is very careful *never* to call Rāma a god, in the roughly *thousand-page* poem—in the Hindu way of thinking (Hindus are sometimes prone to feeling pride in saying that theirs is not a religion in the sense of the Abrahamic ones, but a way of life); translated here by Robert P. Goldman, Sally J. Sutherland Goldman, Rosalind Leferber, Sheldon I. Pollock, and Barend A. van Nooten, and published by Princeton University; it is an unabridged translation of what is known as the Critical Edition of Valmiki's poem in Sanskrit, which sought to arrive at a text as intended and written by the poet himself, even as there are attempts to establish definitive editions of Shakespeare, Dante, Homer, Plato, etc.;

Bible, quran, and bhagavad-gita are beaten to the *malodorous armpits* of their composers by this,

When Rāma arrived with Saumitri at that lake overflowing with lotuses, water lilies, and fish, his passions overflowed, and he lamented. As soon as he saw it, he trembled with rapture. Yielding to that power of love, he said to Saumitri: 'Saumitri, see how lovely the forest is around Lake Pampa. Its crested trees are as splendid as mountains. But anguish still torments me, as I grieve over Bharata's sorrow and the abduction of Vaidehi.

'And yet this grassy plot, deep green and yellow, glistens brightly, carpeted with many-colored blossoms from the trees. With gentle breezes and with blossoms and fruits growing on the trees, this fragrant spring month is a time of heightened passion, Saumitri. And look, Saumitri, beautiful flowering thickets are pouring down showers of blossoms, like clouds releasing showers of rain. Forest trees of every kind, shaken by the force of the wind, are scattering blossoms on the ground among lovely stones. In glades fragrant with honey, where bees hum, a gentle breeze is blowing, cooled by sandalwood trees. The mountains, with beautiful tall trees blossoming near their lovely crests, look as if their peaks were touching. And look at these *karnikara* trees everywhere in full flower; they are like yellow-robed men covered with gold ornaments....

Ramayana, chapter 4, "The Kiskindhakunda," Sarga 1, verses 1-11

(the Goldman *et al.* translation)

I suppose Christians and Jews find the following to be even *better* (a sincere man, he, when praying to his God to advance his *own* political interests: Psalm 17, of David, a Prophet in Islam and in Christianity—see the Book of Acts in the *New Testament*, and Peter's endorsement of that *king* as an authentic *prophet*, like Jeremiah, Isaiah, and Samuel themselves, utterly free from having committed *any* sin, carnal or mortal—, but *not* in Judaism,

[8] Keep me as the apple of the eye, hide me under the shadow of thy wings,

[9] From the wicked that oppress me, from my deadly enemies, who compass me about.

[10] They are inclosed in their own fat: with their mouth they speak proudly.

[11] They have now compassed us in our steps: they have set their eyes bowing down to the earth;

¹² Like as a lion that is greedy of his prey, and as it were a young lion lurking in secret places.

¹³ Arise, O LORD, disappoint him, cast him down: deliver my soul from the wicked, which is thy sword:

¹⁴ From men which are thy hand, O LORD, from men of the world, which have their portion in this life, and whose belly thou fillest with thy hid treasure: they are full of children, and leave the rest of their substance to their babes.

Old Testament, Book of Psalms, the KJV translation

After all, David did *not* leave *his* "substance" to one of *his* "babes": I don't know whether David means by "babes," his *children*, or his *girlfriends/his court's bedmate-slaves*, besides that court intriguer, Bathsheba.

All gods of all religions throughout history—we are aware that Buddhism, strictly speaking, has no God, but merely nature; *however*, in Buddhism, in action, which is all that matters, most practising Buddhists worship, and pray to, Buddha himself, perversely perverting the creator of their creed—have this in common among their believers, that believers believe in an idea that is *merely made aphoristic in bible*, but common to all false religions *that God's ways are not the ways of humans*—**without this** *one* **idea, whether explicitly stated or not,** *not a single human being* **would believe in god(s).**

The *very act of communing with a trusted God* or *god* (s), or a deified Buddha (worshiped as a god by almost *all*

Buddhists), the very act of asking for guidance (or grace or whatever is the term in a particular religion or sect), what is called *love and worship of a beloved (and, perhaps, feared) God*—let alone beseeching him for favors of a material (or relationship or boss/underling situation, son, father) or spiritual (mental distress asked to be relieved)—, this very act of communing *consists* of that one idea that God's ways are not those of humans, *for otherwise it would be understood that* **God is already doing all that one asks for,** and it would seem both redundant and **obscenely disrespectful** to seek guidance of, or communing with, a God for *any* reason.

Q.E.D.

This is the basis, psychologically speaking, of religions flourishing, thousands of them, all claiming to be the only true ones, through the course of world history.

In the quran,

"But any that (in this life) had repented, believed, and worked righteousness, will have *hopes* [emphasis, *mine*] to be among those who achieve salvation. Thy Lord does create and choose as He pleases: no choice have they (in the matter): Glory to Allah! and far is He above the partners they ascribe (to Him)!" (surah 28, verses 67-68),

the Yusuf Ali translation, chosen because 'tis by a Muhammadan born so, though less literally accurate than Asad's or Arberry's.

It is probably out of his utter humility before God that

Muhammad could not envision a Jesus claiming in his own words, "I am the Son of God," however suggestively, implicitly, and indirectly, in Jesus' *own lifetime.*

Hinduism is a monotheistic religion also, with its sole God called, variously, Brahma or Atma: in a corrupted version of Valmiki's poem, the supposed Valmiki, before he begins its composition proper, rebukes a hunter whom he has witnessed killing two happily copulating birds, copulating at the time they are struck down; then Valmiki feels remorse for having given himself up to the "low" passion of anger in fiercely scolding the hunter. Brahma approaches Valmiki then, and tells him that it was Brahma's own anger (!), the gods who cannot be believed, that he forced-transferred it into Valmiki's heart, and in recompense will inspire him to compose a poem that will last forever, *Ramayana* (!!!), or in Homer's more powerful phrase about the war of the Argives to utterly sack Troy, "the fame of which will never die." Gods whose ways are not those of humans. This is the sort of thing that brave Hindus have made of Valmiki's originally pure poem.

Hinduism is strictly a monotheistic religion, unlike Christianity, *with all the trappings* of polytheism. What we see is that polytheistic gods cannot be trusted by an *intelligent, rational* person to carry out their promises. They have *not* created the human solely to take care of humans. You don't know your karma, unlike the peace promised to true believers by a sole God in all popular creeds. Their gods have too many of their own personal concerns, rivalries, and *eroticisms* to care much about their mortal underlings, except falteringly, as Athena does about Odysseus because of Poseidon's rage. When you take the painstaking *breathing exercises regimen* away from the Hindu scripture Bhagavad-Gita there is left only Krishna's *justification of the murders* of kinsmen to Arjuna, through Platonic-level double talk, that the soul is immortal, you cannot kill an immortal thing, therefore when you slay your cousin you are not killing his soul, so go ahead and kill him, it is *dharma* (religious duty-virtue) to do so: *Gandhi*'s favorite among all sacred Hindu texts was not the *peaceful Ramayana*, but *that* interpolation into dthe very violent *Mahabharata*.

A third monotheistic religion, Judaism, has its sickening "holiday" of Passover, *celebrating* the *murders* of *innocent* first-born *children* of Egyptian subjects, when Yahweh should have killed the Pharaoh, *if Yahweh was moral himself.* Of course, he was *not* (I, a Curate, insist he *was*: after all, only Infinite Justice would **command** a virtuous man, a respectable manager at Morgan Lanley named Mr. Abram (known otherwise, in the dark underworld of Mafiadom, as Abraham the Terrible) to *have sex with his wife's slave*, a woman of the name, Hagar, after making his old wife infertile: what Justice! Surely, He deserves to be called the Father of Jesus Himself, the Savior!: the Father, by doing so, was preparing for His last Messenger and Prophet, Muhammad, a descendant of Hagar, as a member of the Quraysh clan, who all claimed to be descendants of that slave-woman; and one adventure of her life is where the Kaaba is now, the *place of the Father and Yahweh and Allah, all three, One, on Earth, and therefore the holiest site in all of judaism, christianity, and islam, by rights*), any more than Homer's goddess, sister-wife of Zeus, Hera, is.

All "believing" Moslems add and have always added the honorific praise *Salalah* etc. after uttering or writing Muhammad's name, even in the smallest mention of it; but they add *"alai salaam,"* only, when naming other "prophets" accepted by them as sent by allah. Now, what does allah *himself* say to *this?*

Say: "We believe in God, and in that which has been bestowed from on high upon us, and that which has been bestowed upon Abraham and Ishmael and Isaac and Jacob and their descendants, and that which has been vouchsafed to Moses and Jesus, and that which has been vouchsafed to **all** *[emphasis, mine] the [other] prophets by their Sustainer:* **we make no distinction between any of them** *[emphasis, mine]. And it is unto Him that we surrender ourselves."*

Quran, surah 2, verse 136

Simply put, by disobeying *their own* god's explicit, *clear*, and unswerving command (remember allah is much wiser and more knowledgeable than any merely created being, angel, jinn, or human, animal or plant, earth or the sun, etc., and cannot be moved from his Will) all moslems in history have condemned themselves to the very Hell they so ardently fear and believe in.

O Confucians, what does your master direct you to do when he calls for worshiping your ancestors, who centuries ago, may have been ingrained evil-doers, spreading iniquities, and practicing them? And why, O

Confucians, does not Confucius, who seems, by his chiding of followers who are not obedient to him personally, who seems by these personable manners to think himself all-wise, in his vanity or pride, not speak of this? Even more important, why did not any Chinese follower of his time ask him this crucial question, if, indeed Chinese culture and intelligence are so to be admired by the rest of the world, as Chinese people think they *more than* deserve to be, and in China itself.

Absurdities

b

A non-Platonic Dialogue on the Eternal War Between the Three Abrahamic Faiths

Peter P. Robertson, Televangelist

At a posh studio in New York, elitist district. Two men, one young, and one middle-aged.

Camera Man: So, you say you can do better than the Pardoner in Chaucer's famous collection of stories in verse.

Robertson: The Canterbury Trash is nothing compared to this. Prerecord this, intersperse recorded audience responses, and broadcast this tomorrow night, with a logo saying LIVE at the bottom of the screen.

Camera Man: Are you sure this is wise?

Robertson: Do as I say. Who has made the billions, you or I?

Camera Man: Anything you say, boss.

Starts recording, Robertson alone at the Table, famous Table, shoes visible (the other host-hostess will be edited in as rejoicingly listening later).

Robertson: As for the infidel Muslims, here is what I say to them. Repent and believe in Christ, take him as your Savior, after you listen to me. The Muslim viewer [*hand emphasis*] *should not waddle on further* with this broadcast *without* explaining convincingly and in detail why a "Book" that claims that all Jews believe Ezra to be the son of God, does not praise Muhammad for implementing Quranic punishments. Did Muhammad ignore Allah's clear command? Did he exist? And since the only honest answer to the latter question is, "No," which rascal's corpse lies decayed in that "holy" crypt? Verily, Allah says in the Quran, the contract is between the individual human and Allah: no intercessors, neither Prophets nor clerics (the latter of which caste seeks to rob Allah of His Power to decide and will), will be allowed by Him: this is in the Quran that Muslims make a point of never relying upon. I shall now quote from *their* Holy Book,

[*Image on screen of the text, voiceover of Robertson reading it*],

"ALLAH - there is no deity save Him, the Ever-Living, the Self-Subsistent Fount of All Being. Neither slumber overtakes Him, nor sleep. His is all that is in the heavens and all that is on earth. Who is there that could intercede with Him, unless it be by His leave? He knows all that lies open before men and all that is hidden from them, whereas they cannot attain to aught of His knowledge save that which He wills [them to attain]. His eternal power overspreads the heavens and the earth, and their upholding wearies Him not. And he alone is truly exalted, tremendous." (Quran, 2: 255)

[*Cut to Robertson at the Table.*]

Robertson: Allah *alone* knows and sustains all, and someone like Muhammad was merely given *the little* that Allah in all His wisdom thought was *needed by Muhammad* to inaugurate Islam: I quote again the extract, "whereas they cannot attain to aught of His knowledge save that which He wills."

Camera Man: Cut. Reverend Robertson, Allah is omniscient, according to that verse 2:255 of Quran you quoted. It may be ascertained, on the basis of this idea of omniscience, that the god of the Old Testament (or of the slightly different Hebrew Bible) is [*hand emphasis*] *an entity apart and distinguishable from the god of* the New Testament, who is implied throughout as omniscient, also.

[*Camera Man takes out a pocket Bible with a flourish, and puts on his reading glasses, this man with 20/20 eyesight, to read the microscript.]*

Camera Man: I read here in Luke 1:

²⁶ And in the sixth month the angel Gabriel was sent from God unto a city of Galilee, named Nazareth,

²⁷ To a virgin espoused to a man whose name was Joseph, of the house of David; and the virgin's name was Mary.

²⁸ And the angel came in unto her, and said, Hail, thou that art highly favoured, the Lord is with thee: blessed art thou among women.

²⁹ And when she saw him, she was troubled at his saying, and cast in her mind what manner of salutation this should be.

³⁰ And the angel said unto her, Fear not, Mary: for thou hast found favour with God.

³¹ And, behold, thou shalt conceive in thy womb, and bring forth a son, and shalt call his name JESUS.

³² He shall be great, and shall be called the Son of the Highest: and the Lord God shall give unto him the throne of his father David:

³³ And he shall reign over the house of Jacob for ever; and of his kingdom there shall be no end.

³⁴ Then said Mary unto the angel, How shall this be, seeing I know not a man?

[35] And the angel answered and said unto her, The Holy Ghost shall come upon thee, and the power of the Highest shall overshadow thee: therefore also that holy thing which shall be born of thee shall be called the Son of God.

[36] And, behold, thy cousin Elisabeth, she hath also conceived a son in her old age: and this is the sixth month with her, who was called barren.

[37] For with God nothing shall be impossible.

[38] And Mary said, Behold the handmaid of the Lord; be it unto me according to thy word. And the angel departed from her.

Robertson: I know that already.

Camera Man: *But* the God of the other part of the bible, Hebrew or Old Testament, is *not* omniscient: in Genesis, he has merely heard the rumor of homosexuality among the denizens of Gomorrah and Sodom, [*hand emphasis, exactly like Robertson's signature one*] *and has to verify this for himself by seeing this "sin"* before destroying those people. I quote from the Good Book. This is Genesis 18:

[20] And the LORD said, Because the cry of Sodom and Gomorrah is great, and because their sin is very grievous;

[21] I will go down now, and see whether they have done altogether according to the cry of it, which is come unto me; and if not, I will know.

²² And the men turned their faces from thence, and went toward Sodom: but Abraham stood yet before the LORD.

²³ And Abraham drew near, and said, Wilt thou also destroy the righteous with the wicked?

²⁴ Peradventure there be fifty righteous within the city: wilt thou also destroy and not spare the place for the fifty righteous that are therein?

²⁵ That be far from thee to do after this manner, to slay the righteous with the wicked: and that the righteous should be as the wicked, that be far from thee: Shall not the Judge of all the earth do right?

²⁶ And the LORD said, If I find in Sodom fifty righteous within the city, then I will spare all the place for their sakes.

²⁷ And Abraham answered and said, Behold now, I have taken upon me to speak unto the LORD, which am but dust and ashes:

²⁸ Peradventure there shall lack five of the fifty righteous: wilt thou destroy all the city for lack of five? And he said, If I find there forty and five, I will not destroy it.

²⁹ And he spake unto him yet again, and said, Peradventure there shall be forty found there. And he said, I will not do it for forty's sake.

³⁰ And he said unto him, Oh let not the LORD be angry, and I will speak: Peradventure there shall thirty be found there. And he said, I will not do it, if I find thirty there.

³¹ And he said, Behold now, I have taken upon me to speak unto the LORD: Peradventure there shall be twenty found there. And he said, I will not destroy it for twenty's sake.

³² And he said, Oh let not the LORD be angry, and I will speak yet but this once: Peradventure ten shall be found there. And he said, I will not destroy it for ten's sake.

³³ And the LORD went his way, as soon as he had left communing with Abraham: and Abraham returned unto his place.

Robertson: I know that passage well, too. I still don't understand. What's your game, old boy!

Camera Man: Have you read before those verses of the Holy Bible? And understood them?

Robertson: Don't you know, I went to Starvard Divinity School of Medicine?

Camera Man: [*brusquely*] Should I say, "Cut" again? For all that was recorded. You will not be taken down by a sex-scandal, old man, like other televangelists of recent years, but all this conversation has been recorded by *my* editor. As a character says in a Shaw play, or a film based on a Bernard Shaw play, "What's $750,000 to you, and what is this footage to me!"

Robertson [*with the smoothest of unction*]: I have been played up like this before already, you know, and have the right answer for a squirt like you.

Camera Man [*a little taken aback*]: You do? What?

Robertson: Tomorrow shall see you and your editor richer by $375,000 apiece. I went to college and divinity school, so I can do the math rather quickly.

Scene II

Reverend Robertson at his lawyer's office, five months later.

Bonyers: You have truly landed in a delicate spot of malfunction on this occasion. Was this your handwriting at that time? Are there other documents in your hand from that time? Is it, I ask for the final time, really your handwriting? Tell me the truth.

Robertson: It is, alas.

Bonyers: What can we do but pay up, in that case? There is no getting around this. Let me read it to you aloud, this letter from your sworn enemy, and let you imagine newsmen and newswomen reading the whole thing, or even excerpts from this draft version of the entry essay you wrote for admission to the Starford School of Philosophy, to television audiences around the country.

Robertson: Because I am so rich, I can sheepishly say, 'tis a checkered background, mine. You must get me—

Bonyers [*interrupting*]:

[*Reads*]

"My dear Reverend Robertson,

If you had not, in a moment of churlish jealousy (so what if he had privily taken advantage of your fiancée's fatal weakness for his good looks and charming address of speech, you really should not have reported his use of crack cocaine to the university authorities), so damaged the prospects your dormmate at college who was thereafter expelled, the dormmate in the dorm where you composed the following, you would not have been exposed now for your merely academic ambitions. Here is a photocopy of your essay, written for admission to Starford University, titled "In Praise of Atheism," for your perusal. I say nothing more, and let nothing be understood by my sending it to you, which I do out of the kindness of my heart."

Bonyers puts the sheet he was reading from on his desk, and reads aloud from the next two, still in his hands.

[*Reads*]

Nice cursive hand, by the way, Peter.

" '

A Comparison
of the
Divine
With a
Believer in the Divine

by Peter P. Robertson, B.A. (Herstham College)

Mr. Matthew, from chapter 26 of his book, *The Gospel According to St. Matthew*, weak in *spirit*, Jesus, in that Holiest of things, spirit,

[36] Then cometh Jesus with them unto a place called Gethsemane, and saith unto the disciples, Sit ye here, while I go and pray yonder.
[37] And he took with him Peter and the two sons of Zebedee, and began to be sorrowful and very heavy.
[38] Then saith he unto them, My soul is exceeding sorrowful, even unto death: tarry ye here, and watch with me.
[39] And he went a little farther, and fell on his face, and prayed, saying, O my Father, if it be possible, let this cup pass from me: nevertheless not as I will, but as thou wilt.
[40] And he cometh unto the disciples, and findeth them asleep, and saith unto Peter, What, could ye not watch with me one hour?

⁴¹ Watch and pray, that ye enter not into temptation: the spirit indeed is willing, but the flesh is weak.

⁴² He went away again the second time, and prayed, saying, O my Father, if this cup may not pass away from me, except I drink it, thy will be done.

⁴³ And he came and found them asleep again: for their eyes were heavy.

⁴⁴ And he left them, and went away again, and prayed the third time, *saying the same words*. [Emphasis, *mine*]

The same weakness, and for a third repetitious time.

The gospel writers all faced *exactly* the same *narrative/logical* problem (it was not even a religious one) that *any other writer* of any other *pure fiction* would have had to face, to tell the invented story of Jesus and his dying "for our sins": how to *present* Jesus as *fully human* and therefore weak and capable of deep suffering, and *at the same time* as the Son and equal of God the Father, so that Jesus would come to be *worshiped*, their all-too-*political* goal, the *worship* of Jesus. They had not the mental resources, or Jesus did not, to overcome this problem of this all-knowing God not knowing that the suffering will be grievous for only a little time, lasting for a few hours *merely*, and that he will be thereafter again fully in charge of his Creation! Why, in the name of the Holy Spirit who aids, does Jesus need to be *cowardly* when he should have been brave, and have been *thinking of* **nothing** *but the* **joyous** *thought that he was saving believers* **for all time**? He should have been *thanking* the Father for an opportunity to do the same, *again and again*, if the Father so wished! And is not the Father one with the Son, a monotheistic religion? A problem that no Christian *can* solve, for 'tis an absurd matter.

Plato, cleverer than Jesus or Mark or Matthew or Luke or John or Paul, has *his* Socrates say, when dying (from the dialogue, *Phaedo*),

"Go," said he [= Socrates], "and do as I say." Crito, when he heard this, signaled with a nod to the boy servant who was standing nearby, and the servant went in, remaining for some time, and then came out with the man who was going to administer the poison [*pharmakon*]. He was carrying a cup that contained it, ground into the drink. When Socrates saw the man he said: "You, my good man, since you are experienced in these matters, should tell me what needs to be done." The man answered: "You need to drink it, that's all. Then walk around until you feel a heaviness | 117b in your legs. Then lie down. This way, the poison will do its thing." While the man was saying this, he handed the cup to Socrates. And Socrates took it in a cheerful way, not flinching or getting pale or grimacing. Then looking at the man from beneath his brows, like a bull—that was the way he used to look at people—he said: "What do you say about my pouring a libation out of this cup to someone? Is it allowed or not?" The man answered: "What we grind is measured out, Socrates, as the right dose for drinking." "I understand," he said, | 117c "but surely it is allowed and even proper to pray to the gods so that my transfer of dwelling [*met-oikēsis*] from this world [*enthende*] to that world [*ekeîse*] should be fortunate. So, that is what I too am now praying for. Let it be this way." And, while he was saying this, he took the cup to his lips and, quite readily and cheerfully, he drank down the whole dose. Up to this point, most of us had been able to control fairly well our urge to let our tears flow; but now when we saw him drinking the poison, and then saw him finish the drink, we could no longer hold back, and, in my case, quite against my own will, my own tears were now pouring out in a flood. So, I covered my face and had a good cry. You see, I was not crying for him, | 117d but at the thought of my own bad fortune in having lost such a comrade [*hetairos*]. Crito, even before me, found himself unable to hold back his tears: so he got up and moved away. And Apollodorus, who had been weeping all along, now started to cry in a loud voice, expressing his frustration. So, he made everyone else break down and cry—except for Socrates himself. And he said: "What are you all doing? I am so surprised at you. I had sent away the women mainly Ie I did not want them | 117e to lose control in this way. You see, I have heard that a man should come to his end [*teleutân*] in a way that calls for measured speaking [*euphēmeîn*]. So, you must have composure [*hēsukhiā*], and you must endure." When we heard that, we were ashamed, and held back our tears. He meanwhile was walking around until, as he said, his legs began to get heavy, and then he lay on his back—that is what the man had told him to do. Then that same man who had given him the poison [*pharmakon*] took hold of him, now and then checking on his feet and legs; and after a while he pressed his foot hard and asked him if he could feel it; and he said that he couldn't; and then he pressed his shins, | 118a and so on, moving further up, thus demonstrating for us that he was cold and stiff. Then he

[= Socrates] took hold of his own feet and legs, saying that when the poison reaches his heart, then he will be gone. He was beginning to get cold around the abdomen. Then he uncovered his face, for he had covered himself up, and said— this was the last thing he uttered— "Crito, I owe the sacrifice of a rooster to Asklepios; will you pay that debt and not neglect to do so?" "I will make it so," said Crito, "and, tell me, is there anything else?" When Crito asked this question, no answer came back anymore from Socrates. In a short while, he stirred. Then the man uncovered his face. His eyes were set in a dead stare. Seeing this, Crito closed his mouth and his eyes. Such was the end [*teleutē*], Echecrates, of our comrade [*hetairos*]. And we may say about him that he was in his time the best [*aristos*] of all men we ever encountered—and the most intelligent [*phronimos*] and most just [*dikaios*].

Askelpios was, of course, dear members of the Academic Admissions Council, a Greek god. Here is an example of a man's death, a man who was *little enough* to believe in his gods and in a *secure* afterlife; and *he did not even include himself as one of those gods*. Socrates' attitude was that of a deeply believing Christian (or Hindu, or Buddhist, or Moslem, etc.) of today, Jesus' was that of a wretched coward.'

Dear Reverend Robertson, I remain, now and ever, your servant,

Geoff C., a bit-player Camera Man"

Robertson: How much is this going to cost me? Not only this, but your never less-than-extravagant fees?

Printed in Great Britain
by Amazon

27089049R00091